T0160857

BOOK 1

CLOTHES. COFFEE. CRUSHES. CRIMES.

PAPERBACK **LA**

A CASUAL ANTHOLOGY

EDITOR
SUSAN LaTEMPA

PROSPECT
·PARK·
BOOKS

Published by Prospect Park Books
2359 Lincoln Ave.
Altadena, CA 91001
www.prospectparkbooks.com

Distributed by Consortium
www.cbsd.com

Library of Congress Cataloging in Publication Data is on file with the Library of Congress. The following is for reference only:

Names: LaTempa, Susan
Titles: Paperback LA (2018)
Identifiers: ISBN 978-1-945551-24-6 (flexibound)
Subjects: Los Angeles, Calif.; anthologies; essays; photography.

Design by Kathy Kikkert
Cover photo: Griffith Observatory, Los Angeles, 2006, by Robert Landau

Printed in Korea

INT. RESTAURANT TERRACE—DAY.

LATER IN THE LUNCH.

TOM: *I'll have a decaf coffee.*

TRUDI: *I'll have a decaf espresso.*

MORRIS: *I'll have a double decaf cappuccino.*

TED: *Do you have any decaffeinated coffee ice cream?*

HARRIS: *I'll have a half-double decaffeinated half-caf. With a twist of lemon.*

TRUDI: *I'll have a twist of lemon.*

TOM: *I'll have a twist of lemon.*

MORRIS: *I'll have a twist of lemon, please.*

CYNTHIA: *I'll have a twist of lemon.*

L.A. STORY

STEVE MARTIN

1991

CONTENTS

SUSAN SONTAG, EVE BABITZ, AND LAWRENCE CLARK POWELL

inspired this anthology, and they've been a trio of angels on my shoulder as I've considered, with Colleen Dunn Bates of Prospect Park Books, what this four-volume series of writing about Los Angeles could be.

The direct inspiration arose one day in the gift shop of the Beverly Hilton Hotel. I was at the hotel for a loooong workday doing my part to organize a fundraising gala. So—frantic work punctuated by waiting. I browsed the shop's plastic Oscar statuettes (tempting), then looked for a book about LA. You know, something to read in bright sunlight by the hotel pool. *Nada.* Nothing to give the visitor a breezy intro. Nothing to give a sense of the intriguing worlds comprising this complex city.

Meanwhile—and this was clearly one of the reasons why I was looking for a book of regional interest in a hotel gift shop—I had been reading Powell's *California Classics: The Creative Literature of the Golden State.*

California Classics is not an anthology but rather a bibliography-style guide, with chapters on each of thirty-one books about California. Powell gives us biography, history, and interpretive criticism that made me want to read at least half of the books described. *California Classics* is out of print, as are many of the books Powell writes about. But as I searched libraries and online sources, I learned that some of the works that were out of print when Powell worked on his book in the late 1960s had returned to print. That was cool.

For more than a decade, Prospect Park Books has employed its "California sensibility" to bring books to the marketplace, so Colleen joined me in the search for what we began to think of as a "casual anthology." We found that although many good anthologies relating to LA have been published, some quite recently, they were either weighty (literally) or quite specialized.

And none included works by Sontag or Babitz. True, only one of Sontag's works, the story "Pilgrimage," is centered in LA. And true, Babitz's novels were out of print for a time. But if a book collecting works of different writers is a kind of conversation, the fact that these two had never been invited to pull up a lawn chair, grab a beer from the ice bucket on the patio, and join the continuous gabfest about LA galvanized me. Someone had to do it.

Once invited, Babitz, the enthusiast, and Sontag, the critic, represented professional attitudes that informed the project and guided our approach to the search and collection of great writing about LA. On one hand, the enthusiast reminds us that to be insightful, you don't need to start from a position that something's wrong. On the other, the critic employs acute observation, specificity, and even charm to convey an experience.

And so another LA colloquy begins. At *Paperback LA* we have the grit and the elbow grease to set out the big table, borrow the folding chairs, string some lights, and pour the drinks. We have the independence and experience to bring folks together from across boundaries of time and history. We know it's a renewal of a conversation hosted by Powell and many others before us, and yet there's still so much to hear about that we have decided to do it again.

And again.

This is the first of four "seatings." Book One of *Paperback LA* features fourteen written pieces, three photo essays, and a collection of quotes. As you turn your paper or electronic pages, you'll be able to eavesdrop as the 1830s Yankee trader "Bill" Davis and the 1950s radical Clancy Sigal compare notes on men's fashions.

You can set aside Waze for a while and explore fantastic new transportation routes described by singer-songwriter Dan Bern and novelist Paul Beatty. Want to get to know the *real* LA? Would that be a teenager's perspective on punk rock in the 1990s, courtesy of contemporary YA writer Cecil Castellucci, or an elderly jockey's view of the latest dance craze in 1915 that comes to us from Harlem Renaissance writer Arna Bontemps?

INTRODUCTION
SUSAN
LaTEMPA

Paperback LA is fortunate to be able to share the first-ever profile of Stanley Rose, a historic figure tantalizingly on the edge of many references to intellectual LA and Hollywood of the 1920s and '30s, brought to center stage here by Victoria Dailey, along with the most famous of our many booksellers, Jacob Zeitlin.

And it's a privilege to make Hugo Reid's scathing 1852 letter to the *Los Angeles Star* more widely available as a stand-alone statement about LA's indigenous residents.

At our imaginary backyard barbecue, the conversations might be casual, but they can also be intense. There are quiet tête-à-têtes, such as one between the immigrant intellectual/pedestrian protagonists of Carlos Bulosan and Héctor Tobar. There are wry exchanges, like the aerial and aural sports poetics of Vin Scully and the Venice Skate Park photographers. Susan Sontag and Robert Landau give nods to European cultural models, and Victor and Mary Lau Valle to Mexican and Spanish ones.

Want to know the *real* LA? Would that be Eve Babitz's homage to sun and surf or Justin Andrew Marks's homage to the women's movement?

Yes, of course.

SUSAN LaTEMPA
LOS ANGELES, 2018

P.S. *Paperback LA* is built on joy, in part because ideas and recommendations from all parts of our lives flow into the conversation. So first of all, we thank our many collaborators throughout our careers in print publications. If you haven't heard from us yet for free advice, you will. Special thanks on this Book One from Susan for hot tips, insights, introductions, material support, and pointed dialogue go to Michael Dawson, Laurel Delp, Patricia and Ryan Mejia, Dan Milder, Irene LaTempa Milder, Richard Natale, Vani Rangachar, Daphna Shalev, Barry Stavro, Richard Stayton, and Kim Wong.

Subtitled "A history of events and life in California: personal, political and military; under the Mexican regime; during the quasi-military government of the territory by the United States, and after the admission of the state to the union: being a compilation by a witness of the events described; a reissue and enlarged illustrated edition of *Sixty Years in California*, to which much new matter by its author has been added which he contemplated publishing under the present title at the time of his death," William Heath Davis's book *Seventy-five years in California* offers eyewitness details of life up and down what is now the state of California. Heath, a wealthy merchant and shipowner, was born in Hawaii and began adult life as a clerk in his uncle's store in San Francisco. He married into the family that held the San Leandro land grant and was an influential resident of San Francisco and later San Diego but traveled extensively, documenting different communities over several decades.

DAPPER DAY CALIFORNIO STYLE

MANNERS AND CUSTOMS OF THE RANCHEROS

WILLIAM HEATH DAVIS

THE CALIFORNIANS WERE EARLY RISERS. THE *RANCHERO* (rancher) would frequently receive a cup of coffee or chocolate in bed, from the hands of a servant, and on getting up immediately order one of the vaqueros to bring him a certain horse which he indicated, every horse in a *caponera* (corral) having a name, which was generally bestowed on account of some peculiarity of the animal. He then mounted and rode off about the rancho, attended by a vaquero, coming back to breakfast between eight and nine o'clock.

This breakfast was a solid meal, consisting of *carne asada* (meat broiled on a spit), beefsteak with rich gravy or with onions, eggs, beans, tortillas, sometimes bread and coffee, the latter often made of peas. After breakfast the ranchero would call for his horse again, usually selecting a different one, not because the first was fatigued, but as a matter of fancy or pride, and ride off again around the farm or to visit the neighbors. He was gone till twelve or one o'clock, when he returned for dinner, which was similar to breakfast, after which he again departed, returning about dusk in the evening for supper, this being mainly a repetition of the two former meals.

Although there was little variety in their food from one day to another, everything was cooked so well and so neatly and made so inviting, the matron of the house giving her personal attention to everything, that the meals were always relished.

When the rancheros thus rode about, during the leisure season, which was between the marking time and the *matanza* or killing time, and from the end of the matanza to the springtime again, the more wealthy of them were generally dressed in a good deal of style, with short breeches extending to the knee, ornamented with gold or silver lace at the bottom, with *botas* (leggings) below, made of fine soft deerskin, well-tanned and finished, richly colored, and stamped with beautiful devices (these articles having been imported from Mexico, where they were manufactured), and tied at the knee with a silk cord, two or three times wound around the leg, with heavy gold or silver tassels hanging below the knee. They wore long vests, with filigree buttons of gold or silver, while those of more ordinary means had them of brass. They wore no long coats, but a kind of jacket of good length, most generally of dark blue cloth, also adorned with filigree buttons. Over that was the long *serape* or *poncho,* made in Mexico and imported from there, costing from twenty to a hundred dollars, according to the quality of the cloth and the richness of the ornamentation.

The serape and the poncho were made in the same way as to size and cut of the garments, but the former was of a coarser texture than the latter, and of a variety of colors and patterns, while the poncho was of dark blue or black cloth, of finer quality, generally broadcloth. The serape was always plain, while the poncho was heavily trimmed with gold or silver fringe around the edges and a little below the collars around the shoulders.

They wore hats imported from Mexico and Peru, generally stiff, the finer quality of softer material, *vicuna,* a kind of beaver skin obtained in those countries. Their saddles were silver-mounted, embroidered with silver or gold, the bridle heavily mounted with silver, and the reins made of the most select hair of the horse's mane, and at a distance of every foot or so there was a link of silver connecting the different parts together.

PHOTO BY JUSTIN ANDREW MARKS

Even today, the Gabrielino/Tongva (Tongva) people, LA's original inhabitants, struggle to be acknowledged, and to save or restore their sacred spaces. These projects include the repatriation and reburial of remains of thousands of ancestors, educational efforts like "UCLA's Mapping Indigenous Los Angeles" website, and culture-preserving work by such groups as the Gabrielino Tongva Springs Foundation.

In 1852, in the early years of American rule of California, a Scots immigrant to Mexican California, Hugo Reid, wrote twenty-two "letters" about "Los Angeles County Indians" to LA's first newspaper, the *Los Angeles Star,* a bilingual (Spanish/English) publication. Reid was a trader who had married Victoria Bartolomea, a member of a leading family of the Gabrielino town Comicranga. She had grown up at the San Gabriel Mission, and it is believed that her family and community contributed to Reid's pointed, sometimes sarcastic reports on the culture, condition, and attitudes of the people whose lands had been taken by successive overlords. The following is his final letter, published July 24, 1852.

FIRST PEOPLES OBSERVED
A LETTER

LOS ANGELES COUNTY INDIANS

HUGO REID

HAVING GIVEN A SKETCH OF THE ANGELES COUNTY INDIANS from the time they were the free, natal possessors of the soil, living contented in a state of nature, until these civilized times of squatting and legislative oppression, in which not only they, but those bearing their blood in a fourth degree, are included, to the shame of this our country . . . I shall now conclude them [the sketches] with a very short review of how far their ancient manners and customs remain in force among the handful left of a once happy people.

Their former lodges [villages] are not now in existence, and most of the Indians remaining in the county are from other parts—from Santa Ynez to San Diego. A few are to be found at San Fernando, San Gabriel, and Los Angeles. Those in service on ranchos are a mere handful. You will find at present more of them in the county of Monterey than in this, excluding those places named above. Death has been busy among them for years past. . . .

I have previously mentioned that their language has deteriorated much since the conquest. Numerous causes affect all languages, and one of the many which did so to theirs was the want of their former Councils held so frequently, in which their wise men spoke with eloquence suited to the occasion, using more dignity and expression, which naturally elevated the [speaking] of all, and gave a tinge of better utterance even in ordinary conversation. They have, at present, two religions—one of custom, and another of faith. Naturally fond of novelty, the Catholic one serves as a great treat—its forms and ceremonies an inexhaustible source of amusement. They don't

14

quarrel with their neighbor's mode of worship, but consider their own the best. The life and death of our Saviour is only, in their opinion, a distorted version of their own life. Hell, as taught them, has no terrors. It is for whites, not Indians, or else their fathers would have known it. The Devil, however, has become a great personage in their sight; he is called "Liza," and makes his appearance on all occasions. Nevertheless, he is only a bugbear and connected with the Christian faith; he makes no part of their own. The resurrection they cannot understand, but a future state of spiritual existence is in accordance with their creed.

Their chiefs still exist. In San Gabriel remain only four, and those young. There are more, but of tribes formerly from the direction of San Bernardino. They have no jurisdiction more than to appoint times for the holding of feasts and regulating affairs connected with the church. No standing church remains nowadays: it is made yearly and consecrated when required, on any spot they choose to select. Their food continues the same, with the addition made to the list of what the Spaniards introduced. Their clothing is of course distinct, and a cloak made of rabbit skins has within this year or two become a novelty among themselves.

For a long time back, marriage has been performed in the Catholic Church; and only one instance of its fulfillment in their own alone exists in the case of a young girl who contracted matrimony about three years ago. Marriage vows, I am sorry to say, are not very binding, although many examples of strict fidelity exist. Women undergo the same purification after child birth as formerly, with the exception of such as were in the service of whites at their first parturition. The seers have declined very much in their ability—both of predicting events and doing harm; although instances of sickness occasionally occur of which they stand the blame. In performing cures, however, they still take the precedence of the other members of the faculty known as MDs.

Years ago, shell bead money was current in the Mission, not only between Indians, but between them and the whites. It is now extremely scarce, and hoarded from one year to another to use at their church ceremonies, and repurchased again for double its value.

I have refrained from touching on politics; administrators I have left to work out their own salvation—and dates, with statistics, I leave to those possessed of abler pens to furnish an account of and of which there is a fine field open to write about—confining myself entirely to the title of these letters. If these sketches of Indian character have been at all interesting to the readers of the *Star*, I shall consider myself amply paid for the time occupied in writing them.

PHOTO BY JUSTIN ANDREW MARKS

On a Facebook page called "Los Angeles Dance Halls and Ballrooms History," you can see a 1921 newspaper clip referring to "the only park on the coast owned and operated by the Race...situated about eight miles out of Los Angeles" with "dancing, boating, swimming, and a merry-go-round." In another clip from the same year, "Leak's Lake in Watts" announces "a moonlight picnic with music by the Spike Bros Novelty Orchestra." The venue, which shows up in music memoirs and histories as a pioneering and integrated jazz scene managed at one point by Jelly Roll Morton, is the model for Green Lake in the novel *God Sends Sunday*. Harlem Renaissance writer Arna Bontemps brings his famous character Little Augie (fashioned on Bontemps's great-uncle) to a somewhat rowdy retirement in Watts, a rural town connected to LA by streetcar. Little Augie was present the day the shimmy came to LA.

WATTS PASTORALE
CIRCA 1915

GOD SENDS SUNDAY

ARNA BONTEMPS

WHILE IN WATTS ON HIS ERRAND FOR LEAH, AUGIE GOT
a bit of news from Mudtown that made a sharp impression on his mind.
It seemed that big doings were cooking in that neighborhood. The railroad
men, Pullman car porters and dining-car waiters, were about to give their
annual picnic and dance. It was an event in those days, an event so popular
with the local blacks that their reports of it filled the old fellow with an excitement keener than he had felt in years. So he immediately determined to go.
But he decided to keep his plans to himself and perhaps surprise the young
folks by his presence. He had felt, of late, that Terry and the Clow girls considered him an old has-been. It would do him good to give them a surprise.
So while the youngsters were making plans to attend he stood apart and kept
his thoughts to himself.

Green Lake, the dance-hall park on the edge of Mudtown, had formerly
been the house and yard of the farmer in whose walnut grove the small neighborhood had sprung up. Now, with flying-horses and a small wooden dance
pavilion, it was the most satisfactory place in the vicinity for the colored out-
ings and dances. Aside from the times when it was secured for such frolics,
it was opened but once a week. On these days Negro and Mexican children
flocked there in Sunday school clothes, enchanted by the painted horses, the
flags, and the little mechanical organ. That one horse lacked a tail and one a
foreleg and that others were losing their manes meant nothing to their ardor.

18

They pressed one another noisily in the line, their tiny fingers perspiring and sticky from grasping pennies.

There was little here to amuse grown-ups. But for the occasion of the railroad men's picnic special preparations were made. A small carnival company set up a row of gaming concessions in canvas tents. The gypsies who usually camped on the fringes of the grove drew near and opened a booth beneath the trees. And, not to be outdone, Negroes came with things to sell: pig's feet, crawdaddies, baked sweet potatoes, corn on the cob, slices of watermelon, lemonade. The odors from their steaming kettles filled the air.

It was afternoon when the big crowd began to arrive. In the clear sunlight their gay clothes made a striking pageant against the green yards of Mudtown. That morning a fog swept the treetops and roof gables, but it passed quickly as the day warmed and the women came with sun parasols and fans. A few of the country folks arrived in wagons and buggies, but the larger part of the crowd walked. Though wearing new shoes, many of which had high heels and were painful, the young women were loud and cheerful.

Terry went with the Clow girls in the late afternoon. But he had been in Mudtown in his Uncle Pig's house all morning and had watched the early ones with great amusement as they passed. In the first rush a young mulattress with enormous hips minced along painfully. A beribboned hat dangled on her arm and ribbons streamed from her shoulders and from her waist. A puny-looking boy, half her size and dull black, escorted her slowly and with commendable patience. At every few paces she paused to rest. She was not one to make a secret of her misery; her feet were bothering her, and as she approached Pig's gate Terry saw that she had perspired freely, the moisture staining her silk dress beneath the arms and on the shoulders.

"I do so hate hot weather," she was telling her companion. "I nachally can't stan' it. It's on 'count o' me bein' so plump-lak, I reckon."

He smiled, showing a little embarrassment. "Tha's a' right, baby. Jes' take it easy; us got plenty o' time. You know them raw-bony gals ain't no good in de wintertime. Tha's when you shines."

"Too, I has a lil trouble wid ma feet. Standin' so much, you know. Some days I be's on ma feet from mawnin' to night. It's mighty hard on we heavyset gals."

"Hm. I on'erstand everything. I'm a Pullman porter maself, an' them movin' trains is sumpin' or other on de dogs too."

Terry thought of the anecdotes he had so often heard the railroading fellows tell among themselves about their feet after a hard run, about having to step off curbstones backwards to avoid pain, or crawling the last few steps home from the depot.

All day the brilliant colors of gaudy clothes flashed in the sun; reds predominated, violent sun-bright shades and the diminishing tones of strawberry, coral, and pink. The same old nigger taste, the same childlike love of color, was everywhere manifest.

Terry met the Clow girls just before sunset. Elbowing their way through the crowds, they began making a round of the booths. White men with hollow faces, tobacco-stained mouths, and hard rasping voices announced their games. Beside them stood stringy, middle-aged women, their faces grotesquely rouged, offering hoops and balls to the Negroes.

Through the lace trees, above the booths, the sunset showed softly. One by one the firm straight light shafts withdrew, leaving the park in shadow. The odors of steaming food stimulated appetites. Terry and the girls bought pig's feet and sat on a bench, away from the biggest crowd, to eat.

As the park darkened, a portion of the folks dispersed. The ironic flying horses of the merry-go-round stopped, their heads still unbent, the exhausted young riders toppled from their backs. It became quite dark; beneath a remote tree where there had been a fire some coals glowed softly, uttering a faint smoke like breath.

Soon afterward the pavilion was lighted and the dance music commenced. When Terry and the girls followed the crowd inside a few couples were already on the floor. They were just warming to the vivid, slow-drag rhythm. The contagion seemed to spread in ripples. Here a toe tapped the floor, a little farther on a finger snapped; one by one the boys reached for the girls. "How 'bout it, honey?"

"Suits me."

"Let's strut."

The couple standing next to Terry got off. The music halted for an instant on a high note as if uncertain—then decided. Clash! The cymbals came sharply together. Beulah took the movement. His arm around her waist, Terry's body made a corresponding curve.

A trombone, its gold throat pointed upward, rose above the other instruments, enlarged its mouth, and cried. Suddenly the rough-board walls lost their security and the floor, dipping and tossing, seemed to float. Unaccustomed to frenzies of this sort, Terry was soon completely intoxicated. In the orchestra he saw the mouth of that horn like a barrel-head. Hidden behind it, the musician became a dwarf. A clarinet stretched the length of a man, and at the piano, the keyboard of which had assumed a crazy angle, two huge disembodied hands worked magic.

Beulah danced with easy grace; she knew the steps, but she was not self-conscious. As they circled the group, Beulah humming the melodies, Terry imagined that he could feel her body vibrate. He imagined that under the influence of music some compulsion other than her own will possessed her and directed her movements. He had often heard of such dancing.

During another dance Terry stood off to the side, steadying himself against a post. In the circle of dancers revolving before him he saw many who were perspiring, their straightened hair beginning already to crimp near the scalp where the moisture touched it. Again the pitiful, half-suppressed pain of tight shoes was everywhere evident.

A lean yellow boy, wearing a candy-striped shirt and a box coat, came over to Terry. When he smiled he exhibited a row of gold teeth. Terry knew that the fellow was easing around in order to dance with Beulah and Azilee. He walked with a slight affectation, appearing to favor one foot. But not in the manner of a lame person.

"Whut's de matter?" Terry asked pleasantly. "Feet hurt?"

"Nah," the boy grinned. "Feet don't hurt; jes' got a lil seam in ma sock."

"It ain't de shoe?"

"Hell, no. Not these here shoes." He put his hands on them. "Looka there—sof' as a glove. Plenty big too; see? It's de damn sock."

Terry did not argue, but he was unconvinced. "You railroadin'?" the yellow boy asked.

Terry shook his head. "Nah. You?"

"Hm. It's de lif. Ma daddy was a railroadin' man too."

Then he introduced himself to Terry: Napoleon Haide.

"They calls me Nappy for shawt," he said. "I'm jes' heah two days this trip. Nice gals out heah."

"You lak 'em?"

"When I says they is right, they is right. I done seen 'em all, from heah to New Yawk."

Terry saw that Nappy's hair and skin were near the same yellow color—what the Negroes call "riney." He had heavy lips, a thick nose, and gray eyes which were inclined to be pink around the edges. His hair, moreover, was very kinky.

"De brown-skinned gal 'cross yonder," Nappy pointed—"is she yo' company?"

"Yeah, I got two," Terry said.

After that the four of them got together, a sort of party to themselves. When Nappy danced his head bent forward above the girl's and even his shoulders seemed to fold around her. Terry thought he was trying to get too much from a dance; he was too avid. But Azilee enjoyed dancing with him, and evidently her thoughts were not the same as Terry's.

In the midst of the noisy whirl, the gay laughter of the young people, the extravagant clothes, when the young folks were least prepared for such a surprise, Augie adjusted his hat and entered the dance pavilion. He stood in the doorway quietly for a moment in his ancient and ruined finery, casting his glances about. He wore the Prince Albert with the vest of faded flowers and with these a pair of outlandish old shoes for which he had improvised laces of red ribbons. He felt arrogant and self-assured, not in the least ashamed, and showed only scorn for the crowd.

Seeing him standing there, Terry and Beulah came across to him at the close of the dance.

"I thought this thing was fancy," Augie sneered.

"Don't you lak it?" Beulah laughed.

"I'm used to fancy niggers, niggers whut would make dis crowd look 'shamed."

"That was when you was a jockey?"

"Hm. An' clo'es! I don't see no clo'es. This heah is a country ring-play. This ain't no dance."

Augie had alcohol on his breath, but he was not drunk. He, of course, was unable to take part in the modern dances. His scorn would not have permitted it anyway.

"I got de hoss an' wagon," he said. "It outside waitin' for you, Miss Beulah. I'll drive y'all gals home when you is through dancin'."

"Thank you, Lil Augie."

"Whut 'bout me?" Terry smiled.

"You an' Miss Azilee betta walk," Augie said. "Y'all betta walk. Me an' Miss Beulah might wanna co't." He punched Terry with his elbow.

In the dances that followed, Terry stood up often in order to keep Augie company. He must have imagined that the old man felt as out of place as he looked. The crowd increased steadily, and the circle became uncomfortably compact. Revolving slowly, it suggested a gaudy pinwheel. Augie amused himself by watching the couples.

A muscular black girl went by in a sleeveless dress and striped stockings. Others followed: a buff-colored girl with a face painted till it resembled porcelain, a short dwarfed girl with incongruous hands and feet dancing with a tall man, a young buck with rubber hips and a distressed woman who held his neck, a bold pair who stood in a shadow writhing, a beautiful brown girl yielding the curves of her body to a hideous-looking man, a stout woman whose preposterous breasts kept her partner at a safe distance.

"Bumpety-bump," someone sang.

"Ah buggie-wuggie!"

Many were perspiring. There was a steady hum of voices. Some place in the mass a woman shouted.

"Oo-wee!"

It was an odd outburst, not unlike those uttered in religious frenzy. A few girls giggled. Most of them were too absorbed even to notice.

Augie saw Terry, dancing with Beulah again, weaving deftly through the compact crowd near the orchestra. Suddenly in the midst of the cauldron something hit the floor with a thump like a dead weight. In the center of a little clearing was the fat woman whom Terry had seen during the afternoon. She was sprawled on the slick floor and laboring with the aid of three men to regain her feet, but those high-heeled shoes were gigantic handicaps. Her little sheepish escort babied her a moment, and they set out again bravely.

Directly in front of the musicians there was a bit of space where the floor was brighter than elsewhere because of the extra lights for the orchestra. Some of the dancers were inclined to hurry past this spot because it put them too much in evidence. Others sought it and lingered there, passing remarks with the musicians. A flashy pair were showing a new dance that they had picked up in the city, on Central Avenue, in some of the less respectable places, and were attracting considerable attention. It was a dance in which the shoulders and hips twitched rhythmically, but in which the feet made no steps.

Couples, seeing them, exchanged meaning glances. Some of the men said things that made the girls giggle.

"Jelly! A-ah jelly! Jelly on a plate!"

"Slow an' easy."

"Now rock lak a boat."

The denizens of Mudtown were seeing the shimmy for the first time in a public place. In those days it was regarded as a low, unseemly dance, and the young country girls felt a little outraged at seeing it done there so boldly. Terry, too, seemed embarrassed and kept trying to work through the crowd, to get a safe distance away.

But Augie watched it calmly from the sidelines. He had nothing but scorn for the modern nigger dances. He thought of the night he walked with Della Green at the Cotton Flower Ball. That had been a real come-off. That was what he called a dance. It was fancy.

Nappy's own girl, a hard-looking scrawny wench with broken front teeth, had been neglected and was now looking for him. Seeing her, Nappy excused himself from his new acquaintances and went where she was standing. The dance was about played out; people were leaving. Terry called Azilee, and with Augie and Beulah they left.

The moon was big outside. Everything else seemed small—the trees, the houses, and the little blue hills in the distance. Augie and Beulah got in the cart, and Augie clucked at Miss Ludy.

The tiny rig wavered and jolted along a whitewashed fence, beneath over-hanging branches, and turned into the big road.

Terry and Azilee followed a footpath to the road. After the poorly venti-lated pavilion and the reek of perspiring dancers, the night air was a blessing. As they walked Terry watched the cart. He could almost cry looking at Augie in his ridiculous mashed-up hat sitting beside Beulah!

A block away the sound of the bleating horns reached them, faint and shrunken like a thing remembered. There was, of course, no pavement in the neighborhood and only a single street lamp above the low houses. With this behind, tall incredible shadows fell before Terry and Azilee, creeping face downward as they walked.

Someone ahead on the path laughed merrily, another couple leaving. Arm in arm the fat mulattress and her slight black companion had forgotten pain. Her shoes tied together and suspended across her shoulder, she padded along comfortably in stockinged feet.

It's not all findable on the internet yet. To fill in the gaps, we still rely on nonfiction writers—you know, the folks who go in person to libraries and archives and actual places and look things up and interview people and collect addresses and anecdotes and letters. Then they build a story out of facts and descriptions and quotes and knowledgeable surmises and interesting juxtapositions. We keep wondering about LA in the pre—Hays Office days when the city wasn't noir yet and so much that was unspoken also didn't get written down, exactly. For *Paperback LA,* Victoria Dailey delved into some open secrets tucked between the lines of histories of LA's once-thriving rare and antiquarian book scene.

CULTURE, BOOKS & BOOZE HISTORY

ALMOST A BUSINESS:
SOME RARE BOOKSHOPS IN LOS ANGELES, 1920–1940

VICTORIA DAILEY

> The book business is almost a business, similar to a bar… one is drunk on books and the other is drunk on whiskey; and in each place they hang around.
> —LOUIS EPSTEIN

NOBODY EVER THINKS OF LOS ANGELES AS

a rare-book town anymore. But for most of the twentieth century, it was one of the best in the world. Supported by private collectors and institutional buyers, a large group of booksellers sold all manner of rare books, and the city became a destination for those on the rare-book trail. Not only is book culture elemental to the literary and art history of Los Angeles during the twentieth century, it is also part of Los Angeles's paradoxical past and shadow history, existing quietly amid the flimflammery of boosters, the ballyhoo of Hollywood, and the outré architecture.

As unexpected as a Los Angeles rare-book legacy may be, even more unpredictable is the fact that it is two Texans who loom large in the city's book lore: Jake Zeitlin and Stanley Rose. Arriving separately from the Lone Star State in the early 1920s, each was devoted to books, and while their styles differed, their charismatic personalities attracted writers, artists, and assorted Hollywood types as both friends and customers. Enjoying the company of creative minds, Zeitlin and Rose became legendary figures at the centers of two distinct groups: one artistic and bohemian, the other fueled by alcohol and male camaraderie. As serious as they were about books, Zeitlin and Rose also loved hanging out, carousing, and partying—and, of course, they knew each other.

Jake Zeitlin (1902–1987) hitchhiked to Los Angeles from Fort Worth in 1925, intending to be a guitar-playing poet. Instead, he became LA's leading rare-book dealer. Over a sixty-year career, he sold books, published small-press editions, and mounted important art exhibits—he gave photographer Edward Weston his first show and was instrumental in jump-starting the careers of many local artists. He was active in many liberal causes throughout his long life, including as a campaign activist in Helen Gahagan Douglas's 1950 senate race against Richard Nixon. Aspects of this rich, creative life have been chronicled by various historians over the years.

Stanley Rose (1899–1954), born in the cattle town of Matador, Texas, arrived in Southern California after serving in World War I and became Hollywood's most notorious bookseller of the 1920s and '30s. He began his career by peddling books out of a suitcase he lugged to the movie studios—books that provided the studios with possible plots. And for those in search of other thrills, he offered pornography and bootleg liquor—his suitcase had a false bottom, and it was the era of Prohibition. He is remembered by book people and film historians as the model for the shady bookshop in his friend Raymond Chandler's *The Big Sleep,* and is mentioned in passing in seminal novels and accounts of the period. Like Zeitlin, Rose was well known by his contemporaries, but unlike him, he has been mostly overlooked in histories, in part because he died fairly young and left few traces, and in part because his reputation was tainted by his alcoholism.

OLD BOOKS, NEW SHOPS

Although Zeitlin and Rose changed the style of LA bookselling, they did not invent it—bookshops had been a part of the city's culture since the 1860s. By the 1880s, when throngs of prosperous, well-educated settlers began arriving in the city during the real estate boom, bookshops began to flourish. The city supported a community of booksellers that developed downtown along and around Sixth Street. Easily accessible by the Pacific Electric interurban railway system whose cars pulled in at the central station at Sixth and Main, shops like those of Ernest Dawson and C. C. Parker provided not only popular literature, including LA's first bestseller by a local author, Horace Bell's *Reminiscences of a Ranger* (1881), but also such rare titles as sixteenth-century books illustrated with woodcuts and first editions of Dickens. Bookselling in Victorian Los Angeles remained sober and steady until the Roaring Twenties, when the rise of the film business created a new location—and a new ambience—for the selling of old and rare books: Hollywood.

The bookshops of the 1920s possessed an alluring mystique mixed with an avant-garde sensibility that was connected to the sexy world of artists, actors, writers, directors, drunks, and raconteurs who were part of Hollywood's subcultures. Just as the movie stars rose to fame, some local booksellers also became celebrated for their colorful lives. Gone were the staid shops of their forefathers; the new generation of booksellers, those born around 1900, created a new way to sell books that mirrored the new era.

Often, the bookshops also contained art galleries, reflecting the owners' cultural cachet, aesthetic interests, and friendships. The stores were like clubhouses for the owners' patrons and friends, hangouts for writers and artists. They were places where ideas were discussed and argued, the conversations often enlivened by illegal hooch, especially during Prohibition. Furthermore, studios looking for new stories on which to base movies bought up loads of novels; they also scooped up art books along with costume and architecture books as source material for films with historic settings.

Stanley Rose opened his first bookstore, the Satyr, in 1925 on Hudson Avenue near Hollywood Boulevard. (Was it a coincidence that the man who became known for his backroom bar selected a satyr as his emblem? But then, it was also the symbol of his astrological sign, Sagittarius.) A year later, when Rose added two partners, the Satyr moved into swank new quarters in a deluxe Spanish-style building at 1622 North Vine, next to the Brown Derby, in the hope of finding customers among the restaurant's Hollywood clientele. It worked.

Jake Zeitlin, who opened his first bookshop in 1928 on Hope Street near Sixth downtown, recalled that the Satyr "really got the cream of Hollywood's book business; they had a spectacular bookshop. Everybody that was coming along in Hollywood was there." Zeitlin's shop, just twelve by eight feet, was no more than a hole in the wall. His friend, the printer and book designer Ward Ritchie, called it "the smallest bookshop in existence." It was found "in the back stairway of a derelict building that may once have been a brothel." This louche location was perfect for Zeitlin, the would-be poet—but he had to pay the bills and found his way to selling books rather than writing them. Lawrence Clark Powell called Zeitlin's shop "a crack in the wall" that was unlike any other bookshop, "a place fragrant with oil of cedar. It was the bookshop of Mr. Z."

The Satyr wasn't alone in Hollywood—the area had many other bookstores, especially on Hollywood Boulevard, including the Hollywood Book

Shop, Louis Epstein's Pickwick Book Shop, Unity Pegues, Esme Ward, and Leonard's. Nearby were at least two shops that specialized in metaphysical and occult books: Verne's on Cahuenga and Ralph Kraum on Sunset. (Kraum was also Ronald Reagan's astrologer—long before Reagan met Nancy.) The Hollywood Book Shop, at Hollywood and Highland, was known for its erudite owner, Odo B. Stade, who led an improbable life of scholarship mixed with adventure—a learned bookseller, he had also been a diplomat, gunrunner, naturalist, silent movie actor, stunt flier, writer, translator, and forest ranger. Stade was very successful, especially with Hollywood collectors, but during the Depression, he sold the shop and began writing, including collaborating on *Viva Villa*, a book based on his experiences in Mexico with Pancho Villa that was sold to MGM, became a successful movie, and was nominated for an Academy Award for Best Picture in 1935.

Book collecting became a favorite pastime of many in the increasingly profitable film business. Actors, directors, and producers had loads of cash, and they built superb collections: Jean Hersholt acquired an extensive collection of Hans Christian Andersen (now at the Library of Congress). Joseph Schildkraut's library contained 17,000 volumes. Ronald Colman was buying up first editions of Shelley, Keats, and Oscar Wilde. Rod La Rocque went in for Dickens, Thackeray, and fine bindings. John Barrymore collected first editions, art books, and books on the sea. Charlie Chaplin bought Greek tragedies and classical literature, while Rudolph Valentino acquired books on costume, arms and armor, and yachting. Some actors were reputed to collect erotica, when they could find it. And it was at the Satyr where their chances were good.

Downtown, Zeitlin's artistic nature and magnetic personality attracted not only customers, but also artists and writers, and after a year, he was able to move to somewhat larger quarters on nearby Sixth Street, on LA's old-book row. Among Zeitlin's friends was architect Lloyd Wright, who designed the new shop and created Zeitlin's distinctive grasshopper logo. Zeitlin chose the grasshopper "because like the grasshopper in Aesop's fable, I fiddled and sang in the summertime and froze and starved in the winter."

VICE ON VINE

In 1930, Stanley Rose had a scandal on his hands when he was convicted for violating copyright laws by publishing a pirated edition of a scatological humor book. Although he published it along with his partners, it was Rose who took the rap since he was the only unmarried partner and without a family to support. Although it wasn't for pornography, it served as a warning to would-be smut peddlers, including Rose, that the law would deal harshly with them. His generosity got him a sixty-day jail term. Still, Rose had connections, and not just in Hollywood.

He immediately contacted a good friend, Carey McWilliams, a young lawyer and writer who became prominent in left-wing causes (chairing the Sleepy Lagoon Defense Committee, for example), and who would write one of the most insightful books ever published on Southern California, *Southern California: An Island on the Land* (1946). McWilliams was able to get Rose released, and he arranged for the partners to buy out Rose's interest.

Rose opened his own bookstore directly across the street from the Satyr—the Stanley Rose Bookshop. As McWilliams recalled: "After a few drinks, Stanley would now and then emerge from the store and, to the amusement of his customers, swagger to the curb, shake his fist at his two former associates across the street, and hurl eloquent Texas curses at them."

Rose was an inveterate roué who loved drinking, hard-boiled writers, and hosting his friends; he became the center of an unusually creative group: writers who were known as much for their novels and Hollywood scripts as for their drinking. Rose provided the drinks—he preferred whiskey sours, without sugar—in his backroom bar to such writers as James M. Cain, John O'Hara, William Saroyan, John Steinbeck, Hans Otto Storm, Nathanael West, and F. Scott Fitzgerald, the subjects of Edmund Wilson's 1941 critical study of California novelists, *The Boys in the Back Room*. Although Wilson does not reveal the location of the "back room," it was common knowledge in Hollywood that it was Rose's. Zeitlin described Rose as "a man who had good friends among the bootleggers. During Prohibition you could always get a drink at Stanley Rose's...if you wanted a drink at any hour of the night, you could always knock on Stanley Rose's back door, and he was there at the back of the shop with a jug."

Rose's was the preferred hangout of many other accomplished writers and actors: William Faulkner, John Barrymore, W. C. Fields, Edward G. Robinson, John Fante, Budd Schulberg, Gene Fowler, Horace McCoy, Dashiell Hammett, Raymond Chandler, and even Marion Davies, who found Rose charming enough to invite him to San Simeon for a weekend. Hedda Hopper called him "Stanley Rogue." Budd Schulberg includes Rose's shop in *What Makes Sammy Run*. Nathanael West mentioned him in *The Day of the Locust*.

But it is in Raymond Chandler's work that Stanley Rose, or at least his bookshop, achieved the greatest fame. In one of the most celebrated scenes in the movie *The Big Sleep* (1946), based on Chandler's novel of 1939, Philip Marlowe, posing as a geeky book collector, enters A. G. Geiger's bookshop and asks the snooty clerk a set of obscure questions about two old books. She fails to answer them properly, revealing that she knows nothing about rare books, thereby setting up the scenario in which she, and the entire bookshop, are exposed as frauds: It is a front for the backroom sale of pornography. (Erotica and pornography are the shadow side of rare books.)

As Chandler described it: "A. G. Geiger's place was a store frontage on the north side of the boulevard [Hollywood Boulevard] near Las Palmas.... The entrance door was plate glass, but I couldn't see much through that either, because the store was very dim." Chandler is said to have based Geiger's shop on his friend Stanley's place, especially since Rose was convicted in the piracy case and was known to sell "dirty books"—and Rose's shop was on Hollywood Boulevard's north side, between Las Palmas and Cherokee.

But Marlowe isn't done. Not finding Geiger at the shop, he goes down the street to the Acme Book Shop, hoping for information on the elusive Geiger. There, he encounters another woman, this time, a comely, intelligent one. Their conversation, with its witty wordplay filled with sexual innuendos, sets another tone for rare bookshops, showing them as places of intrigue where men and women could engage in sexy, bookish banter—with possible romantic results. Hollywood noir and rare bookshops have been intertwined ever since, thanks, in part, to Stanley Rose.

ART & PUBLISHING

"Stanley was the least bookish person I've ever seen and I often wondered whether he ever read a book," recalled artist Fletcher Martin of Rose's Prohibition-era activities. "He ran a shop which was a combination cultural center, speakeasy, and bookie joint. Stanley would get whiskey and/or girls for visiting authors.... The ambience was wonderful, something like your friendly local pool hall. He liked artists and always had a gallery in the back."

One of the first art galleries in Los Angeles to show modern art was the Rudolf Schindler–designed Braxton Gallery, located at 1624 North Vine, just across the street from Rose. It was opened in 1929 by Harry Braxton, a former publicity agent from New York, who, with his wife, screenwriter Viola Brothers Shore, was part of a glamorous Hollywood in-crowd that included Josef von Sternberg, Jack Warner, Darryl Zanuck, Harold Lloyd, Joan Crawford, and many others. Braxton exhibited modern art at a time when it was often disparaged in Los Angeles, but he managed to meet several discerning collectors, including Walter Arensberg and Josef von Sternberg, and he succeeded, for a while. His major achievement was arranging with the pioneering art entrepreneur Galka Scheyer to exhibit the work of the Blue Four: Klee, Kandinsky, Feininger, and Jawlensky. In 1933, after divorcing, Braxton closed the gallery and returned to New York.

Perhaps inspired by Braxton's brief gallery success, and undoubtedly sharing many of the same customers, Rose opened a gallery of his own in October 1934, calling it the Centaur Gallery—the former satyr was now a centaur, and Rose used an image of the half-man/half-horse archer as his logo. Located on Selma near Vine, the Centaur Gallery took over where Braxton left off, exhibiting the work of local and international modern artists. Rose, whose background in art was negligible, had the smarts to hire knowledgeable directors, and the gallery held impressive, well-reviewed exhibitions of work by major artists, including Archipenko, Cézanne, Dalí, Ernst, Gris, Léger, Miró, Picasso, Renoir, and Rouault; he also exhibited photographs by Ansel Adams and Edward Weston, and gave Philip Guston his first show.

Zeitlin's bookshop became a meeting place for literary and artistic people and developed not only as a place to buy books and prints, but also as clubhouse of Modernism. While Stanley Rose attracted writers and serious drinkers, Jake Zeitlin attracted writers and bohemians, more prone to drink wine than whiskey. And while Rose played fast and loose with liquor and copyright laws, Zeitlin took another path. About the time that Rose was in court during his piracy case, Zeitlin had set up a small—and legitimate—publishing concern in 1929, The Primavera Press. Taking its name from the original Spanish for Spring Street, Callé de Primavera, the press specialized in reprinting classic works of California literature and history; it was done in by the Depression in 1936, but during its seven years, The Primavera Press published twenty-six books.

Zeitlin's success led him to move again, and in 1934 he opened a larger shop on Sixth Street, again, designed by Wright. In 1938 he moved again, this time farther west, to a carriage house at Carondelet and Wilshire. Among the artists he exhibited were Edward Weston, Peter Krasnow, Henrietta Shore, Paul Landacre, Rockwell Kent, Diego Rivera, and José Clemente Orozco. Zeitlin's craggy good looks made him an ideal subject, and many of his artist friends, including Weston, Landacre, Will Connell, and Max Yavno, made portraits of him.

In January 1935, Rose moved the bookshop and gallery to a single location at 6661½ Hollywood Boulevard, conveniently located next to Hollywood's prime watering hole and restaurant, Musso & Frank. This was ideal for Rose, who used Musso's bar as an extension of his office while continuing to maintain his own backroom bar at the shop. (It didn't hurt that the offices of the Screen Writers Guild were across the street at Hollywood and Cherokee.) As McWilliams recalled: "Stanley was a superb storyteller and a very funny man whose generosity was proverbial. In the late afternoons, as he began to warm up for the evening with a few drinks, he would hold court in the store, entertaining whoever happened to drop in, and the performance would invariably continue into the early morning hours in the back room at Musso's."

After Rose's gallery director left in 1937, the exhibitions became more modest, with shows of amateur or little-known artists, reflecting Rose's lack of knowledge about art. In 1938, no doubt arranged as an act of kindness by his many friends to keep the gallery afloat, Rose held an exhibition of movie star memorabilia that included such tidbits as a caricature of Charlie Chaplin by child star Jane Withers. One of the gallery's last exhibitions, in June 1939, was of whittled wood figurines by Carl Frim, a Swedish masseur to the stars.

Rose tried to carry on, but as a businessman, he wasn't too careful and his lax habits caught up with him. He lent money to anyone who asked and allowed his pals to charge their book purchases—and many never paid their bills. As Bob Thomas, a reporter with a Hollywood beat, recalled, "The trouble was that Stanley had too many friends. So many of them borrowed books and money that he went out of business." Losing steam, the gallery and bookshop closed at the end of June 1939. Rose had gotten married that April, and moved with his wife to San Bernardino, where her parents lived. There, he tried the simple life by raising tomatoes. It wasn't for him.

By 1941, Rose was back in Hollywood, where he became an agent—with one client, at first, William Saroyan, who offered to sign with him partly because Rose needed the money, but also, as reciprocation for countless meals and drinks, and for the many Saroyan books Rose had sold in his shop. Saroyan had been negotiating at the time with MGM for a contract to write *The Human Comedy*, and received $60,000 plus $1,000 per week. Saroyan gave Rose $10,000 as his cut, more than the usual ten percent, a real act of charity. Rose's drinking was legendary by this time, and the studio used that to its advantage: Whenever a meeting was scheduled at MGM, one of Louis B. Mayer's assistants made sure to give Rose all the whiskey he wanted, rendering him unable to negotiate a contract. According to caricaturist Al Hirschfeld, Mayer once asked Saroyan, "Who the hell is this loafer you bring in with you all the time?" Saroyan replied: "That's my agent."

Rose struggled on, representing a few more clients, including actor and author Audie Murphy and Pat McCormick, a Texas beauty pageant winner who became the first woman bullfighter. (After all, Rose was from Matador, Texas.) Another old friend and fellow Hollywood bookseller, Louis Epstein, let Rose use his Pickwick Bookshop as his mailing address when Rose was living nearby in a seedy hotel. As Rose's drinking became more debilitating, his wife left him, taking their young son with her. Rose died in 1954, broke and alone, a dismal ending for the man who was once the droll center of a dazzling crowd.

By 1948, Jake Zeitlin had enough money to buy his own building, the Red Barn at 815 North La Cienega, in what is now West Hollywood, where he continued to sell books until his death in 1987.

Zeitlin was at the center of so many social and artistic circles in LA, and he had a hand in organizing and encouraging so many creative endeavors, that it's easy to lose track of them all. He helped Frieda Lawrence sell D. H. Lawrence's manuscripts; got screenwriting jobs for Aldous Huxley while publishing two of his books; and he sold to and advised Dr. Elmer Belt as he acquired his massive collection of works by Leonardo da Vinci, now at UCLA. Zeitlin's personal charm, combined with his knowledge of books and art, made him someone book people sought out for sixty years.

How unpredictable, how unexpected, and yet, how like Los Angeles to have had two Texans at the center of its rare-book history. But then, LA, magnetic and receptive, has always attracted eccentrics, dreamers, and mold-breakers. Its reputation—and shadow history—depend on them.

Along with Hawaii and Washington State and Alaska, California is central to the story of colonial and post-colonial Pilipino migration and settlement in the US. It's not (surprise?) a pretty tale. Behind the caricatures of the "Filipino houseboy" employed by Chandler, Faulkner, Steinbeck, and many other novelists and screenwriters was a virulent wave of persistent racism. Decade after decade, white separatists won targeted legislation to work around the legal fact that because the Philippines were an American colony, Pilipinos were American nationals. While at first there were no restrictions on immigration, marriage, and school attendance by Pilipinos in the US, twentieth-century politicians passed discriminatory legislation—and then eventually, perversely, used the 1946 recognition of the independence of the Philippines as an excuse for immigration controls.

Carlos Bulosan, a writer and labor organizer who came to America as a teenager in the early 1930s, is a Pacific Coast history icon. Alaska, San Luis Obispo, and, most significantly, Seattle figure in his 1946 autobiographical novel, *America Is in the Heart.* His "first day in LA" story, with its wrenching contrast between the hunger of the unemployed and the routine lethality of on-duty police, is a potent, personal account of the days in our fair city when your very identity could be illegal. May they never come again.

A DAY'S WORK FICTION?

AMERICA IS IN THE HEART

CARLOS BULOSAN

I REACHED LOS ANGELES IN THE EVENING. AN EARLY AUTUMN rain was falling. I waited in the station, looking among the passengers for Filipino faces. Then I went out and turned northward on Los Angeles Street, and suddenly familiar signs on barber shops and restaurants came to view. I felt as though I had discovered a new world. I entered a restaurant and heard the lonely sound of my dialect, the soft staccato sound of home. I knew at once that I would meet some people I had known in the Philippines.

I sat on one of the stools and waited. I saw three American girls come in with three Filipinos. I thought I knew one of the Filipinos, so I approached him and spoke in Ilocano. But he did not understand me; even when I spoke in Pangasinan, he did not understand me. He was of another tribe, possibly a Visayan.

"If you are looking for your brother," said the proprietor to me, "go to the dance hall. That is where you always find them." I asked him to direct me. It was still early, but the girls were already arriving. They went hastily up the stairs and their perfume lingered after them. I stood outside for a long time watching through the door until the guard closed it.

Filipinos started going inside, putting their hands high above their heads so that the guard could search them for concealed weapons. The guard was a white man and he was very rough with them. I went to Main Street, turned to the north, and found the Mexican district. The sound of Spanish made me feel at home, and I mingled with the drunks and the jobless men. In the old plaza some men were debating a political issue; a shaggy old man was preaching to a motley crowd. And farther down the street, near Olvera Market, I saw little Mexican boys carrying shoeshine boxes. They were eating sunflower seeds and throwing the empty shells into each other's faces.

It was now getting late. The crowd in the street was dispersing. The bells in the church tower began to ring. I looked up and saw devotees coming out of the door. It was already ten o'clock and the night services were over. The haggard preacher in the plaza leaped from his perch and disappeared in the crowd. I sat on a wooden bench and put my cap over my face so that I could sleep in the glare of the street lamps.

Toward midnight a drunk came to my bench and lay down to sleep. I moved away from him, giving him enough space to be comfortable. Then a young Mexican whose voice sounded like a girl's sat beside me. He put his hand on my knee and started telling me about a place where we could get something to eat. I was hungry and cold, but I was afraid of him.

I walked away from him, watching the church across the street. When I was sure no one was looking, I rushed to the door and entered. The church was empty. I went to a comfortable corner and lay on the floor. I saw an old man with a white beard coming in the door, and I thought he saw me. But he went to the candles and blew them out one by one, then disappeared through a side door. It was like heaven, it was so warm and quiet and comfortable. I closed my eyes and went to sleep.

I was awakened in the morning by the merry peals of tiny bells. I ran across the room and through the door, bumping into many people who were arriving for the morning services. I walked in the crowded street toward the Filipino district. I felt as though a beast were tearing at the walls of my stomach. The pain nauseated me: I was hungry again.

I thought I saw my brother Macario in a streetcar. I jumped on with all the power of my legs, but I was wrong. I got out on the next block and started walking aimlessly. I began to wonder if my life would always be one long flight from fear. When had I landed in America? It seemed so long ago. I crossed the green lawn of the new City Hall.

I walked from Main Street to Vermont Avenue, three miles away. I returned to town by streetcar and went to First Street again. A Filipino poolroom was crowded, and I went inside to sit on a bench. The players were betting and once in a while they would give the table boy a dime. I waited until the men started coming in groups, because their day's work was done.

I was talking to a gambler when two police detectives darted into the place and shot a little Filipino in the back. The boy fell on his knees, face up, and expired. The players stopped for a moment, agitated, then resumed playing, their faces coloring with fear and revolt. The detectives called an ambulance, dumped the dead Filipino into the street, and left when an interne and his assistant arrived. They left hurriedly, untouched by their act, as though killing were a part of their day's work.

All at once I heard many tongues speaking excitedly. They did not know why the Filipino was shot. It seemed that the victim was new in the city. I was bewildered.

"Why was he shot?" I asked a man near me.

"They often shoot Pinoys like that," he said. "Without provocation. Sometimes when they have been drinking and they want to have fun, they come to our district and kick or beat the first Filipino they meet."

"Why don't you complain?" I asked.

"Complain?" he said. "Are you kidding? Why, when we complain it always turns out that we attacked them! And they become more vicious, I am telling you! That is why once in a while a Pinoy shoots a detective. You will see it one of these days."

"If they beat me I will kill them," I said.

The Filipino looked at me and walked away. As the crowd was beginning to disperse, I saw the familiar head of my brother Macario. He was entering the poolroom with a friend. I rushed to him and touched his hand. He could not believe that I was in America.

"Why didn't you write that you were coming?" he asked.

"I did not know I was coming, brother," I said. "Besides, I did not know your address. I knew that I would not stop traveling until I found you. You have grown older."

"I guess I have, all right," he said. Then suddenly he became quiet, as though he were remembering something. He looked at me and said, "Let's go to my hotel."

I noticed that he did not speak English the way he used to speak it in the Philippines. He spoke more rapidly now. As I walked beside him, I felt that he was afraid I would discover some horror that was crushing his life. He was undecided what to do when we reached Broadway Street, and stopped several times in deep thought. He had changed in many ways. He seemed in constant agitation, and he smoked one cigarette after another. His agitation became more frightening each minute.

"Why was the Filipino shot?" I asked, pretending not to notice his mental anguish.

"Someday you will understand, Carlos," he said.

Carlos! He had changed my name, too! Everything was changing. Why? And why all this secrecy about the death of one Filipino? Were the American people conspiring against us? I looked at my brother sidelong but said nothing. Suddenly I felt hungry and lonely and tired.

The Broad museum, Downtown LA, 2016

LA
OBSCURA
ROBERT
LANDAU

I started taking pictures as a teenager growing up here in the mid-1960s. I was steadily encouraged by my father, Felix Landau, who had an art gallery on La Cienega Boulevard. At first, I wanted to shoot black-and-white photos like the ones in books my father shared with me by older European photographers with names like André Kertész, Brassaï, and Eugène Atget. Their photographs captured the look and feel of their city (mainly Paris) in direct, poetic, and often unexpected ways—even when confronting scenes that appeared banal and ordinary. To me these books presented pictures taken over lifetimes and seen together, are more meaningful than seen individually. Images from diverse settings and different time periods are unified by an evolving personal sensibility. That's how I've come to see the body of work on LA I've created. This style is sometimes called street photography or urban landscape, but to me it's a form of visual autobiography composed of notes and observations. The photographs are un-manipulated and weave together elements of documentary photography and photojournalism, but my approach relies more heavily on a personal narrative for dictating what and how to photograph.

Quite early on I became aware of how important color is in portraying Los Angeles. Color is an essential element, often the subject itself. Another subject is how clever and artful this city can be in creating surfaces and façades designed to catch the passing eye and draw attention with very little regard for how long they may last. Also, during most of the time these photographs were being made, Los Angeles had its own particular look and cultural identity. In some ways it still does, and that's part of what I'm after. In my photographs dilapidated signs carry as much weight as public statues, and a new art museum excites me no more than a truly unique laundromat. Both fuel my own essential understanding and appreciation of the Los Angeles I've come to know and have tried to define over the decades. That's what I'm really after.

—R.L.

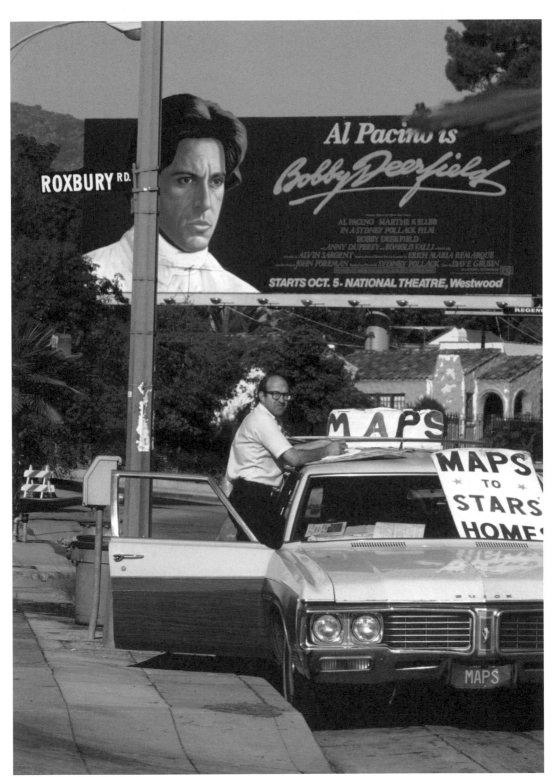

Pacino Billboard/Maps to Stars, Sunset Strip, 1977

Plane Crash Set, Universal Studios, 2007

The Starlet, Burbank, 2011

Bike Path, Santa Monica, 1986

Auto, East LA, 1989

The Farmers Market, 2015

Floating Bush, West LA, 2015

Red Truck/Purple Wall, West LA, 2009

The Standard Hotel, Sunset Strip, 2016

Superman Billboard, Sunset Strip, 1980

She and her best friend are willing to die for Igor Stravinsky, but he's not the subject of this memoir. She hangs out at Pickwick Book Shop on Hollywood Boulevard and attends chamber-music concerts. She rides the Chandler Avenue trolley through a city of "lemon trees and beach boys and neo-Bauhaus architecture and fantasy hamburgers." You may not recognize Susan Sontag's 1947 Los Angeles, but it was real.

TEEN IDOL
A MEMOIR

PILGRIMAGE

SUSAN SONTAG

EVERYTHING THAT SURROUNDS MY MEETING WITH HIM

has the color of shame.

December, 1947. I was fourteen, steeped in vehement admirations and impatience for the reality to which I would travel once released from that long prison sentence, my childhood.

End almost in sight. Already in my junior year, I'd finish high school while still fifteen. And then, and then…all would unfold. Meanwhile I was waiting, I was doing time (still fourteen!), recently transferred from the desert of southern Arizona to the coastland of southern California. Another new setting, with fresh possibilities of escape—I welcomed that. My peripatetic widowed mother's remarriage, in 1945, to a handsome, bemedalled, and be-shrapnelled Army Air Forces ace who'd been sent to the healing desert to cap a year-long hospitalization (he'd been shot down five days after D-Day) appeared to have grounded her. The following year our newly assembled family—mother, stepfather, kid sister, dog, notionally salaried Irish nanny left over from the old days, plus the resident alien, myself, had vacated the stucco bungalow on a dirt road on the outskirts of Tucson (where we'd been joined by Captain Sontag) for a cozy shuttered cottage with rosebush hedges and three birch trees at the entrance of the San Fernando Valley, where I was currently pretending to sit still for a facsimile of family life and the remainder of my unconvincing childhood. On weekends my now out-of-uniform but still militarily perky stepfather marshaled sirloins and butter-brushed corn tightly wrapped in tinfoil on the patio barbecue; I ate and ate—how could I not, as I watched my morose, bony mother fiddling with her food? His animation was as threatening as her apathy. They couldn't start playing family now— too late! I was off and running, even if I looked every inch the baby-faced, overgrown elder daughter effusively munching her fourth ear of corn; I was already gone. (In French one can announce, while lingering unconscionably, *Je suis moralment partie*.) There was just this last bit of childhood to get past. For the duration (that wartime locution that gave me my first model of con-descending to present time in favor of the better future), for the duration it was permissible to appear to enjoy their recreations, avoid conflict, gobble their food. The truth was, I dreaded conflict. And I was always hungry.

I felt I was slumming, in my own life. My task was to ward off the drivel (I felt I was drowning in drivel)—the jovial claptrap of classmates and teachers, the maddening bromides I heard at home. And the weekly comedy shows festooned with canned laughter, the treacly Hit Parade, the hysterical narrat-ings of baseball games and prize fights—radio, whose racket filled the living room on weekday evenings and much of Saturday and Sunday, was an endless torment. I ground my teeth, I twirled my hair, I gnawed at my nails, I was polite. Though untempted by the new, tribal delights of suburban childhood that had quickly absorbed my sister, I didn't think of myself as a misfit, for I assumed my casing of affability was being accepted at face value. (Here the fact that I was a girl seeps through.) What other people thought of me remained a dim consideration, since other people seemed to me astonishingly unseeing as well as uncurious, while I longed to learn everything: the exasper-ating difference between me and everyone I'd ever met—so far. I was certain there was a multitude like me, elsewhere. And it never occurred to me that I could be stopped.

If I didn't mope or sulk, it was not just because I thought complaining wouldn't do any good. It was because the flip side of my discontent—what, indeed, throughout my childhood had made me so discontented—was rap-ture. Rapture I couldn't share. And whose volume was increasing steadily: since this last move I was having near-nightly bouts of jubilation. For in the eight houses and apartments of my life before this one I had never had a bed-room to myself. Now I had it, and without asking. A door of my own. Now I could read for hours by flashlight after being sent to bed and told to turn off the light, not inside a tent of bedclothes but outside the covers.

I'd been a demon reader from earliest childhood (to read was to drive a knife into their lives), and therefore a promiscuous one: fairy tales and comics (my comics collection was vast), Compton's Encyclopedia, the Bobbsey Twins and other Stratemeyer series, books about astronomy, chemistry, China, biographies of scientists, all of Richard Halliburton's travel books, and a fair number of mostly Victorian-era classics. Then, drifting to the rear of a stationery and greeting-card store in the village that was downtown Tucson in the mid-nineteen-forties, I toppled into the deep well of the Modern Library. Here were standards, and here, at the back of each book, was my first list. I had only to acquire and read (ninety-five cents for the small ones, a dollar twenty-five for the Giants)—my sense of possibility unfolding, with each book, like a carpenter's rule. And within a month of arriving in Los Angeles I tracked down a real bookstore, the first of my bookstore-besotted life: the Pickwick, on Hollywood Boulevard, where I went every few days after school to read on my feet through some more of world literature—buying when I could, stealing when I dared. Each of my occasional thefts cost me weeks of self-revilement and dread of future humiliation, but what could I do, given my puny allowance? Odd that I never thought of going to a library. I had to acquire them, see them in rows along a wall of my tiny bedroom. My household deities. My spaceships.

Afternoons I went hunting for treasure: I'd always disliked going home directly from school. But in Tucson, visits to the stationery store excepted, the most cheering postponement I'd come up with was a walk out along the Old Spanish Trail toward the Tanque Verde foothills, where I could examine close up the fiercest saguaros and prickly pears, scrutinize the ground for arrowheads and snakes, pocket pretty rocks, imagine being lost or a sole survivor, wish I were an Indian. Or the Lone Ranger. Here in California there was a different space to roam and I had become a different Lone Ranger. Most days after school I boarded the trolley on Chandler Avenue to hasten into, not away from, town. Within a few blocks of the enchanted crossroads of Hollywood Boulevard and Highland Avenue lay my little agora of one- and two-story buildings: the Pickwick; a record store whose proprietors let me spend hours each week in the listening booths, gorging myself on their wares; an international newsstand where militant browsing yielded me *Partisan Review, Kenyon Review, Sewanee Review, Politics, Accent, Tiger's Eye, Horizon*; and a storefront through whose open door one afternoon I unselfconsciously trailed two people who were beautiful in a way I'd never seen, thinking I was entering a gym, which turned out to be the rehearsal quarters of the dance company of Lester Horton and Bella Lewitzky. O golden age! It not only was,

I knew it was. Soon I was sipping at a hundred straws. In my room I wrote imitation stories and kept real journals; made lists of words to fatten my vocabulary, made lists of all kinds; played conductor to my records; read myself sore-eyed each night.

And soon I had friends, too, and not very much older than myself—to my surprise. Friends with whom I could speak of some of what absorbed and enraptured me. I didn't expect them to have read as much as I had; it was enough that they were willing to read the books I lent them. And in music, even better, I was the novice—what bliss! It was my desire to be taught, even more thwarted than my desire to share, that made me my first friends: two seniors at whom I flung myself soon after entering this new school as a sophomore, whose taste in music was far superior to mine. Not only were they each proficient on an instrument—Elaine played the flute, Mel the piano—but they had done all their growing up here, in southern California, with its infusion of refugee virtuosi, employed in the full symphony orchestras maintained by the major film studios, who could be heard at night playing the canonical and the contemporary chamber repertory to small gatherings scattered across a hundred miles. Elaine and Mel were part of that audience, with tastes elevated and made eccentrically rigorous by the distinct bias of high musical culture in Los Angeles in the nineteen-forties—there was chamber music, and then there was everything else. (Opera was so low on the scale of musical goodness it was not worth mentioning.)

Each friend was a best friend—I knew no other way. Besides my music mentors, who started at UCLA the following autumn, there was a fellow sophomore, my romantic comrade for the remaining two years of high school, who was to accompany me to the college I had already elected at thirteen as my destiny—the College of the University of Chicago. Peter, fatherless and a refugee (he was part Hungarian, part French), had had a life even more marked by displacements than my own. His father had been arrested by the Gestapo, and Peter and his mother escaped Paris to the South of France and from there, via Lisbon, to New York in 1941; after a spell in a Connecticut boarding school, he was now reunited here with the very single, tanned, red-haired Henya (whom I acknowledged to be as young-looking, if not as beautiful, as my own mother). Our friendship started in the school cafeteria with an exchange of boastful anecdotes about our glamorously dead fathers. Peter was the one with whom I argued about socialism and Henry Wallace, and with whom I held hands and wept through *Open City, Symphonie Pastorate, The Children of Paradise, Mädchen in Uniform, The Baker's Wife, Brief*

Encounter, and *Beauty and the Beast* at the Laurel, the theatre we'd discovered that showed foreign movies. We went bicycling in the canyons and in Griffith Park and rolled about, embracing, in the weeds—Peter's great loves, as I remember, were his mother, me, and his racing bicycle. He was darkhaired, skinny, nervous, tall. I, though always the youngest, was invariably the tallest girl in the class and taller than most of the boys and, for all my outlandish independence of judgment on matters Olympian, on the matter of height had the most abjectly conventional view. A boyfriend had to be not just a best friend but taller, and only Peter qualified.

The other best friend I made, also a sophomore, though at another high school, and also to enter the University of Chicago with me, was Merrill. Cool and chunky and blond, he had all the trappings of "cute," a "dish," a "dreamboat," but I, with my unerring eye for loners (under all disguises), had promptly seen that he was smart, too. Really smart. Therefore capable of separateness. He had a low, sweet voice and a shy smile and eyes that smiled sometimes without his mouth—Merrill was the only one of my friends I doted on. I loved to look at him. I wanted to merge with him or for him to merge with me, but I had to respect the insuperable barrier: he was several inches shorter than I was. The other barriers were harder to think about. He could be secretive, calculating (even literally so: numbers figured often in his conversation), and sometimes, to me, insufficiently moved by what I found moving. I was impressed by how practical he was, and how calm he remained when I got flustered. I couldn't tell what he really felt about the quite plausible family—mother, real father, younger brother (who was something of a math prodigy), even grandparents—with which he came equipped. Merrill didn't like to talk about feelings, while I was seething with the desire to express mine, preferably by focusing feeling away from myself onto something I admired or felt indignant about.

We loved in tandem. Music first—he'd had years of piano. (His brother played the violin, which made me equally envious, though it was for piano lessons that I'd implored my mother—rather, stopped imploring my mother—years before.) He introduced me to getting into concerts free by ushering (at the Hollywood Bowl in the summer), and I made him a regular at the Monday chamber-music series "Evenings on the Roof," to which I'd been brought by Elaine and Mel. We were building our nearly identical, ideal record collections (on 78s, happily unaware that this was the last year before LPs), and joined forces often in the cool, dark listening booths of the Highland Record Store. Sometimes he came to my house, even if my parents were there. Or I went to his house; the name of his frumpy, hospitable mother—I remember finding this embarrassing—was Honey.

Our privacy was in cars. Merrill had a real driver's license, while mine was the "junior" license one could hold from fourteen to sixteen in California then, entitling me to drive my parents' cars only. Since parents' cars were the only ones available to us, the difference was moot. In his parents' blue Chevy or my mother's green Pontiac we perched at night on the rim of Mulholland Drive, the great plain of twinkling lights below like an endless airport, oblivious of the mating couples in cars parked around us, pursuing our own pleasures. We pitched themes at each other in our inexact treble voices: "Okay, listen. Now, what's this?" We quizzed each other's memory of Köchel listings, knowing by heart long stretches of the six hundred and twenty-six. We debated the merits of the Busch and the Budapest Quartets (I'd become an intolerant partisan of the Budapest); discussed whether it would be immoral, given what I'd heard from Elaine and Mel about Gieseking's Nazi past, to buy his Debussy recordings; tried to convince ourselves that we had liked the pieces played on the prepared piano by John Cage at last Monday's "Evenings on the Roof" concert; and talked about how many years to give Stravinsky.

This last was one of our recurrent problems. Toward John Cage's squawks and thumps we were deferential—we knew we were supposed to appreciate ugly music; and we listened devoutly to the Toch, the Krenek, the Hindemith, the Webern, the Schoenberg, whatever (we had enormous appetites and strong stomachs). But it was Stravinsky's music we sincerely loved. And since Stravinsky seemed grotesquely old (we had actually seen him on two Mondays in the small auditorium of the Wilshire Ebell, when Ingolf Dahl was conducting something of his), our fears for his life had given rise to a compelling fantasy à deux about dying for our idol. The question, a question we discussed often, was: what were the terms of the sacrifice we so relished contemplating? How many more years of life for Stravinsky would justify our dying now, on the spot?

Twenty years? Obviously. But that was easy and, we agreed, too good to hope for. Twenty years granted to the ancient homely person we saw Stravinsky to be—that was simply an unimaginably large number of years to the fourteen-year-old I was and the sixteen-year-old Merrill was in 1947. (How lovely that I.S. lived even longer than this.) To insist on getting Stravinsky twenty more years in exchange for our lives hardly seemed to show our fervor.

Fifteen more years? Of course.

Ten? You bet.

Five? We began to waver. But not to agree seemed like a failure of respect, of love. What was my life or Merrill's—not just our paltry California-high-school students' lives but the useful, achievement-strewn lives we thought were awaiting us—compared to making it possible for the world to enjoy five years more of Stravinsky's creations? Five years, okay.

Four? I sighed. Merrill, let's go on.

Three? To die for only three additional years?

Usually we settled on four—a minimum of four. Yes, to give Stravinsky four more years either one of us was prepared right then and there to die.

Reading and listening to music: the triumphs of being not myself. That nearly everything I admired was produced by people who were dead (or very old) or from elsewhere, ideally Europe, seemed inevitable to me.

I accumulated gods. What Stravinsky was for music Thomas Mann became for literature. At my Aladdin's cave, at the Pickwick, on November 11, 1947—taking the book down from the shelf just now, I find the date written on the flyleaf in the italic script I was then practicing—I bought *The Magic Mountain.*

I began it that night, and for the first few nights had trouble breathing as I read. For this was not just another book I would love but a transforming book, a source of discoveries and recognitions. All of Europe fell into my head—though on condition that I start mourning for it. And tuberculosis, the faintly shameful disease (so my mother had intimated) of which my hard-to-imagine real father had died so long ago and exotically elsewhere, but which seemed, once we moved to Tucson, to be a commonplace misfortune—tuberculosis was revealed as the very epitome of pathetic and spiritual interest! The mountainhigh community of invalids with afflicted lungs was a version—an exalted version—of that picturesque, climate-conscious resort town in the desert with its thirty-odd hospitals and sanatoriums to which my mother had been obliged to relocate because of an asthma-disabled child: me. There on the mountain, characters were ideas and ideas were passions, exactly as I'd always felt. But the ideas themselves stretched me, enrolled me in turn: Settembrini's humanitarian élan but also Naphra's gloom and scorn. And mild, good-natured, chaste Hans Castorp, Mann's orphaned protagonist, was a hero after my own unprotected heart, not least because he was an orphan and because of the chastity of my own imagination. I loved the tenderness, however diluted by condescension, with which Mann portrays him as a bit simple, overearnest, docile, mediocre (what I considered myself to be, judged by real standards). Tenderness. What if Hans Castorp was a Goody Two-Shoes (appalling accusation my mother had once let fly at me)? That was what made him not like but unlike the others. I recognized his vocation for piety; his portable solitude, lived politely among others; his life of onerous routines (that guardians deem good for you) interspersed with free, passionate conversations—a glorious transposition of my own current agenda.

For a month the book was where I lived. I read it through almost at a run, my excitement winning out over my wish to go slowly and savor. I did have to slow down for pages 334 to 343, when Hans Castorp and Clavdia Chauchat finally speak of love, but in French, which I'd never studied: unwilling to skip anything, I bought a French-English dictionary and looked up their conversation word by word. After finishing the last page, I was so reluctant to be separated from the book that I started back at the beginning and, to hold myself to the pace the book merited, reread it aloud, a chapter each night.

The next step was to lend it to a friend, to feel someone else's pleasure in the book—to love it with someone else, and be able to talk about it. In early December I lent *The Magic Mountain* to Merrill. And Merrill, who would read immediately whatever I pressed on him, loved it, too. Good. Then Merrill said, "Why don't we go see him?" And that's when my joy turned to shame.

Of course I knew he lived here. Southern California in the nineteen-forties was electric with celebrity presences for all tastes, and my friends and I were aware not only of Stravinsky and Schoenberg but of Mann, of Brecht (I'd recently seen *Galileo*, with Charles Laughton, in a Beverly Hills theatre), and also of Isherwood and Huxley. But it was as inconceivable that I could be in contact with any of them as that I could strike up a conversation with Ingrid Bergman or Gary Cooper, who also lived in the vicinity. Actually, it was even less possible. The stars stepped out of their limos onto the klieg-lighted sidewalk of Hollywood Boulevard for the movie-palace premiere, braving the surge of besieging fans penned in by police sawhorses; I saw newsreels of these apparitions. The gods of high culture had disembarked from Europe to dwell, almost incognito, among the lemon trees and beach boys and neo-Bauhaus architecture and fantasy hamburgers; they weren't, I was sure, supposed to have something like fans, who would seek to intrude on their privacy. Of course, Mann, unlike the other exiles, was also a public presence. To have been as officially honored in America as Thomas Mann was in the late nineteen-thirties and early nineteen-forties was probably more improbable than to have been the most famous writer in the world. A guest at the White House, introduced by the Vice President when he gave a speech at the Library of Congress, for years indefatigable on the lecture circuit, Mann had the stature of an oracle in Roosevelt's *bien-pensant* America, proclaiming the absolute evil of Hitler's Germany and the coming victory of the democracies. Emigration had not dampened his taste, or his talent, for being a representative figure. If there was such a thing as a good Germany, it was now to be found in this country (proof of America's goodness), embodied in his person; if there was a Great Writer, not at all an American notion of what a writer is, it was he.

But when I was borne aloft by *The Magic Mountain*, I wasn't thinking that he was also, literally, "here." To say that at this time I lived in southern California and Thomas Mann lived in southern California—that was a different sense of "lived," of "in." Wherever he was, it was where-I-was-not. Europe. Or the world beyond childhood, the world of seriousness. No, not even that. For me, he was a book. Books, rather—I was now deep in *Stories of Three Decades*. When I was nine, which I did consider childhood, I'd lived for months of grief and suspense in *Les Misérables*. (It was the chapter in which Fantine is obliged to sell her hair that had made a conscious socialist of me.) As far as I was concerned, Thomas Mann—being, simply, immortal—was as dead as Victor Hugo.

Why would I want to meet him! I had his books.

I didn't want to meet him. Merrill was at my house, it was Sunday, my parents were out, and we were in their bedroom sprawled on their white satin bedspread. Despite my pleas, he'd brought in a telephone book and was looking under "M."

"You see? He's in the telephone book."

"I don't want to see!"

"Look!" He made me look. Horrified, I saw: 1550 San Remo Drive, Pacific Palisades.

"This is ridiculous. Come on—stop it!" I clambered off the bed. I couldn't believe Merrill was doing this, but he was.

"I'm going to call." The phone was on the night table on my mother's side of the bed.

"Merrill, please!"

He picked up the receiver. I bolted through the house, out the always unlocked front door, across the lawn, beyond the curb to the far side of the Pontiac, parked with the key in the ignition (where else would you keep the car keys?), to stand in the middle of the street and press my hands to my ears, as if from there I could have heard Merrill making the mortifying, unthinkable telephone call.

What a coward I am, I thought, hardly for the first or the last time in my life; but I took a few moments, hyperventilating, trying to regain control of myself, before I uncovered my ears and retraced my steps. Slowly.

The front door opened right into the small living room, done up with the Early American "pieces," as my mother called them, that she was now collecting. Silence. I crossed the room into the dining area, then turned into the short hall that went past my own room and the door of my parents' bathroom into their bedroom. The receiver was on the hook. Merrill was sitting on the bed's edge, grinning.

"Listen, that's not funny," I said. "I thought you were really going to do it."

He waved his hand.

"I did."

"Did what?"

"I did it." He was still smiling.

"Called?"

"He's expecting us for tea next Sunday at four."

"You didn't actually call!"

"Why not?" he said. "It went fine."

"And you spoke to him?" I was close to tears. "How could you?"

"No," he said, "it was his wife who answered."

I extracted a mental picture of Katia Mann from the photographs I'd seen of Mann with his family. Did she, too, exist? Perhaps, as long as Merrill hadn't actually spoken to Thomas Mann, it wasn't so bad. "But what did you say?"

"I said we were two high-school students who had read Thomas Mann's books and would like to meet him."

No, this was even worse than I imagined—but what had I imagined?

"That's so…so dumb!"

"What's dumb about it? It sounded good."

"Oh, Merrill.…"

I couldn't even protest anymore. "What did she say?"

"She said, 'Just a minute, I'll get my daughter,' " Merrill continued proudly. "And then the daughter got on, and I repeated—"

"Go slower," I interrupted. "His wife left the phone. Then there was a pause. Then you heard another voice.…"

"Yeah, another woman's voice—they both had accents—saying, 'This is

Miss Mann, what do you want?'"

"Is that what she said? It sounds as if she was angry."

"No, no, she didn't sound angry. Maybe she said, 'Miss Mann speaking.' I don't remember, but, honest, she didn't sound angry. Then she said, 'What do you want?' No, wait, it was, 'What is it that you want?'"

"Then what?"

"And then I said . . . you know, that we were two high-school students who had read Thomas Mann's books and wanted to meet him—"

"But I don't want to meet him!" I wailed.

"And she said," he pushed on stubbornly, "'Just a minute, I will ask my father.' Maybe it was 'Just a moment, I will ask my father.' She wasn't gone very long . . . and then she came back to the phone and said—these were her words exactly—"

'My father is expecting you for tea next Sunday at four.'"

"And then?"

"She asked if I knew the address."

"And then?"

"That was all. Oh . . . and she said goodbye."

I contemplated this finality for a moment before saying, once more, "Oh, Merrill, how could you?"

"I told you I would," he said.

Getting through the week, awash in shame and dread. It seemed a vast impertinence that I should be forced to meet Thomas Mann. And grotesque that he should waste his time meeting me.

Of course I could refuse to go. But I was afraid this brash Caliban I'd mistaken for an Ariel would call on the magician without me. Whatever the usual deference I had from Merrill, it seemed he now considered himself my equal in Thomas Mann worship. I couldn't let Merrill inflict himself unmediated on my idol. At least, if I went along I might limit the damage, head off the more callow of Merrill's remarks. I had the impression (and this is the part of my recollection that is most touching to me) that Thomas Mann could be injured by Merrill's stupidity or mine . . . that stupidity was always injuring, and that as I revered Mann it was my duty to protect him from this injury.

Merrill and I met twice during the week after school. I had stopped reproving him. I was less angry; increasingly, I was just miserable. I was trapped. Since I would have to go, I needed to feel close to him, make common cause, so we would not disgrace ourselves.

Sunday came. It was Merrill who collected me in the Chevy, at one exactly, in front of my house at the curb (I hadn't told my mother or anyone else of this invitation to tea in Pacific Palisades), and by two o'clock we were on broad, empty San Remo Drive, with a view of the ocean and Catalina Island in the distance, parked some two hundred feet up from (and out of sight of) the house at 1550.

We had already agreed on how we would start. I would talk first, about *The Magic Mountain*, then Merrill would ask the question about what Thomas Mann was writing at present. The rest we were going to work out now, in the two hours we'd allotted to rehearse. But after a few minutes, unable to entertain any idea of how he might respond to what we were considering saying, we ran out of inspiration. What does a god say? Impossible to imagine.

So we compared two recordings of *Death and the Maiden* and then veered to a favorite notion of Merrill's about the way Schnabel played the "Hammerklavier," a notion which I found wonderfully clever. Merrill seemed hardly to be anxious at all. He appeared to think that we had a perfect right to bother Thomas Mann. He thought that we were interesting—two precocious kids, minor-league prodigies (we knew neither of us was a real prodigy, which was someone like the young Menuhin; we were prodigies of appetite, of respect, not of accomplishment); that we could be interesting to Thomas Mann. I did not. I thought we were . . . pure potentiality. By real standards, I thought, we hardly existed.

The sun was strong and the street deserted. In two hours only a few cars passed. Then, at five minutes to four, Merrill released the brake and we coasted silently down the hill and reparked in front of 1550. We got out, stretched, made encouraging mock-groaning sounds to each other, closed the car doors as softly as we could, went up the pathway, and rang the bell. Cute chimes. Oh.

A very old woman with white hair in a bun opened the door, didn't seem surprised to see us, invited us in, asked us to wait a minute in the dim entryway—there was a living room off to the right—and went down a long corridor and out of sight.

"Katia Mann," I whispered.

"I wonder if we'll see Erika," Merrill whispered back.

Absolute silence in the house. She was returning now. "Come with me, please. My husband will receive you in his study."

We followed, almost to the end of the narrow dark passageway, just before the staircase. There was a door on the left, which she opened. We followed her in, turning left once more before we were really inside. In Thomas Mann's study.

I saw the room—it seemed large and had a big window with a big view—before I realized it was he, sitting behind a massive, ornate, dark table. Katia Mann presented us. Here are the two students, she said to him, while referring to him as Dr. Thomas Mann; he nodded and said some words of welcome. He was wearing a bow tie and a beige suit, as in the frontispiece of *Essays of Three Decades*—and that was the first shock, that he so resembled the formally posed photograph. The resemblance seemed uncanny, a marvel. It wasn't, I think now, just because this was the first time I'd met someone whose appearance I had already formed a strong idea of through photographs. I'd never met anyone who didn't affect being relaxed. His resemblance to the photograph seemed like a feat, as if he were posing now. But the full-figure picture had not made me imagine him as frail; it had not made me see the sparseness of the mustache, the whiteness of the skin, the mottled hands, the unpleasantly visible veins, the smallness and amber color of the eyes behind his glasses. He sat very erectly and seemed to be very, very old. He was in fact seventy-two.

I heard the door behind us close. Thomas Mann indicated that we were to sit in the two stiff-backed chairs in front of the table. He lit a cigarette and leaned back in his chair.

And we were on our way.

He talked without prompting. I remember his gravity, his accent, the slowness of his speech: I had never heard anyone speak so slowly. I said how much I loved *The Magic Mountain.*

He said it was a very European book, that it portrayed the conflicts at the heart of European civilization.

I said I understood that.

What had he been writing, Merrill asked.

"I have recently completed a novel which is partly based on the life of Nietzsche," he said, with huge, disquieting pauses between each word. "My protagonist, however, is not a philosopher. He is a great composer."

"I know how important music is for you," I ventured, hoping to fuel the conversation for a good stretch.

"Both the heights and the depths of the German soul are reflected in its music," he said.

"Wagner," I said, worried that I was risking disaster, since I'd never heard an opera by Wagner, though I'd read Thomas Mann's essay on him.

"Yes," he said, picking up, hefting, closing (with his thumb marking the place), then laying down, open again, a book that was on his worktable. "As you see, at this very moment I am consulting Volume IV of Ernest Newman's excellent biography of Wagner." I craned my neck to let the words of the title and the author's name actually hit my eyeballs. I'd seen the Newman biography at the Pickwick.

"But the music of my composer is not like Wagner's music. It is related to the twelve-tone system, or row, of Schoenberg."

Merrill said we were both very interested in Schoenberg. He made no response to this. Intercepting a perplexed look on Merrill's face, I widened my eyes encouragingly.

"Will your novel appear soon?" Merrill asked.

"My faithful translator is at work on it now," he said.

"H. T. Lowe-Porter," I murmured—the first time I'd actually said this entrancing name, with its opaque initials and showy hyphen.

"For the translator this is, perhaps, my most difficult book," he said. "Never, I think, has Mrs. Lowe-Porter been confronted with such a challenging task."

"Oh," I said, having not imagined H. T. L.-P. to be anything in particular but surprised to learn that the name belonged to a woman.

"A deep knowledge of German is required, and much ingenuity, for some of my characters converse in dialect. And the Devil—for, yes, the Devil himself is a character in my book—speaks in the German of the sixteenth century," Thomas Mann said, slowly, slowly. A thin-lipped smile. "I'm afraid this will mean little to my American readers."

I longed to say something reassuring, but didn't dare.

Was he speaking so slowly, I wondered, because that was the way he talked? Or because he was talking in a foreign language? Or because he thought he had to speak slowly—assuming (because we were Americans? because we were children?) that otherwise we wouldn't understand what he was saying?

"I regard this as the most daring book I have written." He nodded at us. "My wildest book."

"We look forward very much to reading it," I said. I was still hoping he'd talk about *The Magic Mountain*.

"But it is as well the book of my old age," he went on. A long, long pause. "My *Parsifal*," he said. "And, of course, my *Faust*." He seemed distracted for a moment, as if recalling something. He lit another cigarette and turned slightly in his chair. Then he laid the cigarette in an ashtray and rubbed his mustache with his index finger; I remember I thought his mustache (I didn't know anyone with a mustache) looked like a little hat over his mouth. I wondered if this meant the conversation was over.

But, no, he went on. "I remember the fate of Germany"…"the demonic" and "the abyss"…and "the Faustian bargain with the Devil." Hitler recurred several times. (Did he bring up the Wagner-Hitler problem? I think not.) We did our best to show him that his words were not wholly lost on us.

At first I had seen only him, awe at his physical presence blinding me to the room's contents. Now I was starting to see more. For instance, what was on the rather cluttered table: pens, inkstand, books, papers, and a nest of small photographs in silver frames, which I saw from the back. Of the many pictures on the walls, I recognized only a signed photograph of FDR with someone else—I seem to remember a man in uniform—in the picture. And books, books, books in the floor-to-ceiling shelves that covered two of the walls. To be in the same room with Thomas Mann was thrilling, enormous, amazing. But I was also hearing the siren call of the first private library I had ever seen.

While Merrill carried the ball, showing that he was not entirely ignorant of the Faust legend, I was trying, without making the divagations of my glance too obvious, to case the library. As I expected, almost all the books were German, many in sets, leather-bound; the puzzle was that I could not decipher most of the titles (I didn't know of the existence of *Fraktur*). The few American books, all recent looking, were easy to identify in their bright, waxy jackets.

Now he was talking about Goethe.…

As if we had indeed rehearsed what we would say, Merrill and I had found a nice, unstrained rhythm of putting questions whenever Thomas Mann's glacial flow of words seemed to be drying up, and of showing our respectful appreciation of whatever he was saying. Merrill was being the Merrill I was so fond of: calm, charming, not stupid at all. I felt ashamed that I'd assumed he would disgrace himself, and therefore me, in front of Thomas Mann. Merrill was doing fine. I was, I thought, doing so-so. The surprise was Thomas Mann, that he wasn't harder to understand.

I wouldn't have minded if he had talked like a book. I wanted him to talk like a book. What I was obscurely starting to mind was that (as I couldn't have put it then) he talked like a book review.

Now he was talking about the artist and society, and he was using phrases

I remembered from interviews with him I had read in *The Saturday Review of Literature*, a magazine I felt I'd outgrown since discovering the fancy prose and convoluted arguments of *Partisan Review*, which I had just started buying at the newsstand on Hollywood Boulevard. But, I reasoned, if I found what he said now a little familiar it was because I had read his books. He couldn't know he had in me such a fervent reader. Why should he say anything he hadn't already said? I refused to be disappointed.

I considered telling him that l loved *The Magic Mountain* so much that I had read it twice, but that seemed silly. I also feared he might ask me about some book of his which I had not read, though so far he hadn't asked a single question. "*The Magic Mountain* has meant so much to me," I finally ventured, feeling that it was now or never.

"It sometimes happens," he said, "that I am asked which I consider to be my greatest novel."

"Oh," I said.

"Yes," said Merrill.

"I would say, and have so replied recently in interviews.…" He paused. I held my breath. "*The Magic Mountain*." I exhaled.

The door opened. Relief had come: the German wife, slowgaited, bearing a tray with cookies, small cakes, and tea, which she bent over to set down on a low table in front of the sofa against one wall. Thomas Mann stood up, came around the table, and waved us toward the sofa; I saw he was very thin. I longed to sit down again, and did, next to Merrill, where we'd been told to sit, as soon as Thomas Mann occupied a wing chair nearby. Katia Mann was pouring tea from a heavy silver service into three delicate cups. As Thomas Mann put his saucer on his knee and raised the cup to his mouth (we followed, in unison), she said a few words in German to him in a low voice. He shook his head. His reply was in English—something like "It doesn't matter" or "Not now." She sighed audibly, and left the room.

Ah, he said, now we will eat. Unsmiling, he motioned to us to help ourselves to the cakes.

At one end of the low table that held the tray was a small Egyptian statuette, which sits in my memory as a funerary votive figure. It reminded me that Thomas Mann had written a book called *Joseph in Egypt*, which in the course of a cursory browsing at Pickwick I'd not found enticing. I resolved to give it another try.

No one spoke. I was aware of the intense, dedicated quiet of the house, a quiet I had never experienced indoors; and of the slowness and self-consciousness of each of my gestures. I sipped my tea, tried to control the crumbs from the cake, and exchanged a furtive glance with Merrill. Maybe it was over now.

Putting down his cup and saucer, then touching the corner of his mouth with the edge of his thick white napkin, Thomas Mann said that he was always pleased to meet American young people, who showed the vigor and health and fundamentally optimistic temper of this great country. My spirits sank. What I had dreaded—he was turning the conversation to us.

He asked us about our studies. Our studies? That was a further embarrassment. I was sure he hadn't the faintest idea what a high school in southern California was like. Did he know about Drivers' Education (compulsory)? Typing courses? Wouldn't he be surprised by the wrinkled condoms you spotted as you were darting across the lawn for first period (the campus was a favorite nighttime trysting spot)—my own surprise having revealed, the very first week I entered, my being two years younger than my classmates, because I'd witlessly asked someone why there were those little balloons under the trees? And by the tea being sold by a pair of pachukes (as the Chicano kids were called) stationed along the left wall of the assembly building every morning recess? Could he imagine George, who, some of us knew, had a gun and got money from gas-station attendants? Ella and Nella, the dwarf sisters, who led the Bible Club boycott that resulted in the withdrawal of our biology textbook? Did he know Latin was gone, and Shakespeare, too, and that for months of tenth-grade English the visibly befuddled teacher handed out copies of the *Reader's Digest* at the beginning of period—we were to select one article and write a summary of it—then sat out the hour in silence at her desk, nodding and knitting? Could he imagine what a world away from the Gymnasium in his native Lübeck, where fourteen-year-old Tonio Kröger wooed Hans Hansen by trying to get him to read Schiller's *Don Carlos*, was North Hollywood High School, alma mater of Farley Granger and Alan Ladd? He couldn't, and I hoped he would never find out. He had enough to be sad about—Hitler, the destruction of Germany, exile. It was better that he not know how really far he was from Europe.

He was talking about "the value of literature" and "the necessity of protecting civilization against the forces of barbarity," and I said, yes, yes . . . my conviction that it was absurd for us to be there—what, all week, I'd expected to feel—at last taking over. Earlier, we could only say something stupid. Actually having tea, the social ritual that gave a name to the whole proceeding, created new opportunities for disgrace. My worry that I would do something clumsy was driving out of my head whatever I might have ventured to say.

I remember beginning to wonder when it would not be awkward to leave. I guessed that Merrill, for all the impression he gave of being at ease, would be glad to go, too.

And Thomas Mann continued to talk, slowly, about literature. I remember my dismay better than what he said. I was trying to keep myself from eating too many cookies, but in a moment of absent-mindedness I did reach over and take one more than I had meant to. He nodded. Have another, he said. It was horrible. How I wished I could just be left alone in his study to look at his books.

He asked us who our favorite authors were, and when I hesitated (I had so many, and I knew I should mention only a few) he went on—and this I remember exactly: "I presume you like Hemingway. He is, such is my impression, the most representative American author."

Merrill mumbled that he had never read Hemingway. Neither had I; but I was too taken aback even to reply.

How puzzling that Thomas Mann should be interested in Hemingway, who, in my vague idea of him, was a very popular author of novels that each had been made into romantic movies (I loved Ingrid Bergman, I loved Humphrey Bogart) and wrote about fishing and boxing (I hated sports). He'd never sounded to me like a writer I ought to read. Or one my Thomas Mann would take seriously. But then I understood it wasn't that Thomas Mann liked Hemingway but that we were supposed to like him.

Well, Thomas Mann said, what authors do you like?

Merrill said he liked Romain Rolland, meaning *Jean-Christophe*. And Joyce, meaning *Portrait of the Artist*. I said I liked Kafka, meaning *Metamorphosis* and *In the Penal Colony*, and Tolstoy, meaning the late religious writings as much as the novels; and, thinking I must cite an American because he seemed to expect that, threw in Jack London (meaning *Martin Eden*).

He said that we must be very serious young people. More embarrassment. What I remember best is how embarrassing it was.

I was still worrying about Hemingway. Should I read Hemingway?

He seemed to find it perfectly normal that two local high-school students should know who Nietzsche and Schoenberg were…and up to now I'd simply rejoiced in this first foretaste of the world where such familiarity was properly taken for granted. But now, it seemed, he also wanted us to be two young Americans (as he imagined them); to be, as he was (as, I had no idea why, he thought Hemingway was), representative. I knew that was absurd.

The whole point was that we didn't represent anything at all. We didn't even represent ourselves—certainly not very well.

Here I was in the very throne room of the world in which I aspired to live, even as the humblest citizen. (The thought of saying that I wanted to be a writer would no more have occurred to me than to tell him I breathed. I was there, if I had to be there, as admirer, not as aspirant to his caste.) The man I met had only sententious formulas to deliver, though he was the man who wrote Thomas Mann's books. And I uttered nothing but tongue-tied simplicities, though I was full of complex feeling. We neither of us were at our best.

Strange that I don't recall how it ended. Did Katia Mann appear and tell us that our time was up? Did Thomas Mann say he must return to his work, receive our thanks for granting this audience, and take us to the study door? I don't remember the goodbyes—how we were released. Our sitting on the sofa having tea and cakes cross-fades in my memory to the scene in which we are out on San Remo Drive again, getting into the car. After the dark study, the waning sun seemed bright: it was just past five-thirty.

Merrill started the car. Like two teenage boys driving away after their first visit to a brothel, we evaluated our performance. Merrill thought it was a triumph. I was ashamed, depressed, though I agreed that we hadn't made total fools of ourselves.

"Damn, we should have brought the book," Merrill said, as we neared my neighborhood, breaking a long silence. "For him to sign."

I gritted my teeth and said nothing.

"That was great," said Merrill, as I got out of the car in front of my house.

I doubt we spoke of it again.

Ten months later, within days of the appearance of the much-heralded *Doctor Faustus* (Book of the Month Club selection, first printing over a hundred thousand copies), Merrill and I were at the Pickwick, giddily eyeing the piles of identical books stacked on a metal table in the front of the store. I bought mine and Merrill his; we read it together.

Acclaimed as it was, his book didn't do as well as Thomas Mann expected. The reviewers expressed respectful reservations, his American presence began to deflate slightly. The Roosevelt era was really over and the Cold War had started. He began to think of returning to Europe.

I was now within a few months of my big move, the beginning of real life. After January graduation, I started a term at the University of California at

Berkeley, luckless George started doing his one-to-five at San Quentin, and in the fall of 1949 I left Cal and entered the University of Chicago, accompanied by Merrill and by Peter (both of whom had graduated in June), and studied philosophy, and then, and then . . . I went on to my life, which did turn out to be, mostly, just what the child of fourteen had imagined with such certitude.

And Thomas Mann, who had been doing time here, made his move. He and his Katia (who had become American citizens in 1944) were to leave southern California, returning to the somewhat leveled magic mountain of Europe, for good, in 1952. There had been fifteen years in America. He had lived here. But he didn't really live here.

Years later, when I had become a writer, when I knew many other writers, I would learn to be more tolerant of the gap between the person and the work. Yet even now the encounter still feels illicit, improper. In my experience deep memory is, more often than not, the memory of embarrassment.

I still feel the exhilaration, the gratitude for having been liberated from childhood's asphyxiations. Admirations set me free. And embarrassment, which is the price of acutely experienced admiration. Then I felt like an adult, forced to live in the body of a child. Since, I feel like a child, privileged to live in the body of an adult. The zealot of seriousness in me, because it was already full-grown in the child, continues to think of reality as yet-to-be. Still sees a big space ahead, a far horizon. Is this the real world? I still ask myself that, forty years later . . . as small children ask repeatedly, in the course of a long, tiring journey, Are we there yet? Childhood's sense of plenitude was denied me. In compensation, there remains, always, the horizon of plenitude, to which I am borne forward by the delights of admiration.

I never told anyone of the meeting. Over the years I have kept it a secret, as if it were something shameful. As if it happened between two other people, two phantoms, two provisional beings on their way elsewhere: an embarrassed, fervid, literature-intoxicated child and a god in exile who lived in a house in Pacific Palisades.

PHOTO BY ROBERT LANDAU

When Clancy Sigal died in July 2017 at the age of ninety, he was professor emeritus (journalism) at USC, having made his way back to LA in 1984 after three decades in England. He had just published *Black Sunset,* his gonzo memoir of life as a young talent agent in mid-1950s Hollywood, when a pair of FBI guys tailed him constantly just as the golden era was morphing into the blacklist era. There were obits in the New York, Los Angeles, and London newspapers, but an appreciation by LA author and professor of politics Peter Dreier was much more to the point, describing how, in his 1961 National Book Award—nominated novel *Going Away,* Sigal conveyed a "love of life, fighting spirit, and sense of adventure" that made it impossible for his fictional alter ego to sink into despair even as he was escaping the country. Sigal's life story reads like a survivor's guide by a Zelig whose Muses are Humor and Outrage. As a nineteen-year-old GI, he went AWOL to attend the Nuremberg trials, intent on assassinating Goering. As a Red Scare refugee in England, he engaged in experimental LSD therapy with psychiatrist R. Laing and had a four-year relationship with novelist Doris Lessing that provided fictional fodder for them both. But some of his weirdest days were during his stint at the Sam Jaffe Talent Agency, "a three-story white stucco Ocean Liner Moderne building at 8553 Sunset Boulevard between Ciro's and Macambo nightclubs."

DAPPER DAY

BLACKLIST-ERA STYLE

BLACK SUNSET:
HOLLYWOOD SEX, LIES, GLAMOUR, BETRAYAL, AND RAGING EGOS

CLANCY SIGAL

SOCRATES IN TASSELED LOAFERS

After I tangle with Sandy at La Rue's, word spreads through Jaffe that I might be a keeper. The imprimatur comes in the form of veteran agents—"Zack Silver," "Jonathan Buck," and "Ace Kantor"—taking me under their wing.

Zack (Navy, minesweeper, Atlantic), affable and almost supernaturally laid-back—the office nice guy—is the inhouse classics scholar, an outdoorsman who hunts with rifle, knife, and crossbow, and is married to a Native American woman with fishing rights on the Puyallup River. Jonny Buck (Colonial Club, Princeton) is mandated to teach me negatives like how not to tread on other agents' turf, how not to take producers' insults personally, how not to make a clumsy visual presentation of myself, above all how not to be a pain in the ass to Jonny himself. He is a barefaced anti-Semite. ("You went to school where? JEWCLA? That explains it.") Ace Kantor (Marines, Pacific), former tennis semi-pro, deals hyper-smoothly with marquee-brand actors and directors. Through Ace I will meet-and-greet most of Jaffe's A-list actors. He is life-greedy, avaricious, collegial, and extraordinarily handsome in the George Hamilton style.

Each senior agent will waste a day on me.

"No matter what you hear, this is an honest business. Crooks don't last long. Short-term you can screw somebody on a deal but the word gets out that you're untrustworthy. In the long run, it doesn't pay off. And it's the payoff that counts." — Zack Silver

"Right away the executives I deal with at Metro and Fox will mistake you for the mail boy. Look how you're dressed! *Schmatte*-ville. Padded shoulders! If you're not prepared to invest in a Brooks Brothers suit, wool, no synthetic drek like Dacron, narrow shoulders, three-inch lapels, get out of the business. I'll send you to my tailor. Genial works—look at Zack—but arrogance is better—look at me. They respect anyone who looks down on them. Don't worry, you'll figure out your own style . . . God help us." — Jonathan Buck

"Go silent, go stealthy, don't draw fire. Smile even if they're throwing bricks at you. Be careful where you laugh. Show respect even to toads. These are very insecure men you're dealing with. You have the goods, they have the money, it's only haggling, goes back to the Egyptians, I'll sell you my camel for your daughter. Trust is everything. Lose a deal rather than lose their trust in you. It's okay to lie to your clients about possibilities because nobody likes bad news. Keep hope alive. Remember: never bury a client just because they look dead. You're Doctor Frankenstein, your job is to bring the monster back to life with your personal magnetism. If they change agents after you make them rich, it doesn't mean they're ungrateful, just Hollywood humans in a jungle on fire. You don't play tennis? Pity. You lift weights? Honey, this ain't Muscle Beach." — Ace Kantor

• • •

For a raw recruit like me the San Fernando Valley studios—Universal, Warners, and Republic—are a boot camp to make my mistakes. As the newest agent I'm also assigned extra shit work, going in cold at sub-Poverty Row outlets like Monogram and its sister Allied Artists and Eagle-Lion and any dinky offices located in the grubby end of Hollywood where fly-by-night producers hang their shingles by the week and pay fifty bucks a script if the writer is lucky. The agent I replaced, "Flip Edwards" (*nee* Feivel Eisenberg), sallow, smelling of Old Kentucky, unshaven, rumpled suit, aggressively depressed—a dramatic contrast to the rest of us—has been exiled to the industry's Siberia, in the shadow of Bekins-type concrete warehouses in parts of Hollywood no star would be seen dead in, because Sam and Mary don't have the heart to fire their only employee who publicly suffers from war nerves eight years after his war is over. He's the only agent to wear in his lapel the tiny brass insignia GIs call the ruptured duck to indicate honorable discharge.

"See these teeth, New Boots?" Flip counsels me in a grubby little diner. "In the squad they called me the Smiler. Face in the shit under an eighty-eight barrage, hey I'm still laughing. Ever been under a tree burst? We told replacements like you to walk point in the Ardennes, why get used to their names. You never even made it across? (Long sigh) Well, you walk point now. Don't bother to knock, walk right in and keep smiling and talk them stories, don't leave them anything to read, most of them never got past the third grade. I love it down here. Nobody's buckin' for promotion. End of the line, New Boots."

· · ·

Each Jaffe agent cultivates a "selling" voice, a form of ventriloquism. We're actors reciting lines from a script depending on whether delivering good or bad news, or if we're inebriated (often), or to intimidate. Just the way you pick up the phone is a self portrait. ("Clancy here—kill for the sake of killing! Who's this?") Walking through the office in the early evening as agents roll up client calls is like listening to fourteen radio dramas at once.

Whenever I'm through with this job, I wonder if Orson Welles might hire me for his *Mercury Theatre on the Air* to play any role required.

GANGSTER CHIC

Mary Baker is a fashion führer. "Goddammit, Clancy, are those argyle socks? Give me a break, you're not a campus cutie anymore!" Meaning, it's time to toss Ray's throwaways and Dress for Success.

A few streets up from the office, at 8804 Sunset where it curves away from West Hollywood, Jaffe has an arrangement with the gangster-haberdasher-and-florist-as-a-front Mickey Cohen, armed robber, killer-to-order—and Ben Siegel's bodyguard until Jack Dragna or Meyer Lansky had Bugsy's face shot off on Linden Drive just around the corner from Mary Baker's mansion. For show and cover, Mickey operates, among other legit businesses, a men's clothing store on the Strip. Even though it exposes him to drive-by assassination, Cohen is a publicity hog who enjoys loitering outside his shop waving to passing tourists. A starfucker, he extends discounts to Jaffe agents in return for access to premieres and parties where he and his bodyguards can mix with movie stars.

Mrs. Baker doesn't trust me to shop alone so one morning sends her two enforcers, my mentors Zack Silver and Jonny Buck, into Mickey's shop to supervise a makeover. At the front door, as in a Grade-B film, a toothpick-chewing bodyguard in an open-necked yellow silk shirt and immaculately pressed trousers eye-frisks us before he lets us in to meet the man himself. Meyer Harris Cohen, "Mickey," emerges from behind a wheeled rack of jackets and empty hangers in a double-wide-shouldered, off-white gabardine suit and his trademark custom-made Joy Lord Hatter of New York fedora, all vain muscle and five o'clock shadow. He's on his way to a four-year prison stretch, but you'd never know it from his demeanor.

Without a word to Zack and Jonny, like a real bespoke tailor, Mickey circles as if I'm a boxer in the ring with him. Pug-busted nose, serious bowlegs, formidable jowls, he sets himself like the featherweight pro fighter that he was, against pretty good opponents I'm told.

"So," he rumbles to style-maven Jonny, "Ivy League or *proster chamoole?*" What's that? I ask. Zack says, "Basically low-class shithead."

Must establish my personal credibility with LA's most notorious crook.

"Mr. Cohen, I ran numbers after school for Max Glauber the bookie." Quick as a flash Mickey responds, "Yeah? You lie." I go, "Cigar store. Roosevelt Road by Homan." Real Chicagoans always say 'by,' not at or near. Jonny and Zack look at me in surprise. Cohen appraises me a long moment, then smiles broadly. We're bonded in Chicago graft.

"Come," he gestures me into the back room, "and you guys jerk off a while."

An hour later I emerge splendiferous in a three-button double-breasted pinstriped Brooks Brothers suit, Collezioni handmade tie with mother-of-pearl tie bar, Armani diamond-design white silk shirt, and Roger Vivier penny loafer oxblood shoes—some of the clothes labeled, some not, all obviously having fallen off the back of a truck, while in a box under my arm I carry a single-breasted two-button glen plaid Savile Row ensemble plus cardigan ("Cary Grant loves that slim Continental style," gushes Mickey), all to match under his careful eye. In the full-length mirror, I look like a mafia lawyer. Zack and Jonny simply stare.

His arm around me, Mickey walks me out of the store and wishes me all the luck in the world.

He bestows upon me a classic Chicago benediction. He says, "Kid, go out there and kill 'em."

Leaving Mickey's establishment in a new suit, shirt, tie, and even shoes makes me feel a thousand percent different. A new man. A company guy. The mask fits.

PHOTO BY POOJA DISSANYAKE, AGE 15/VENICE ARTS

It's not surprising that Eve Babitz's books are returning to print more than forty years after they first appeared. She's one of those artists who is so right about so many of her observations—about light, and air, and the sky and human behavior—that when she offers fictionalized reports of, say, 1958 from the vantage of the early '70s, the reader trusts and honors her words. And now with again more distance from those decades in which she originally published, her work's literary strengths are even more appreciated, in concert with her rare gift for communicating joy in worldly things. Many of us simply bask in her ability to capture a moment. It is so damned hard to find the right words to transport readers (*transport?* It even sounds hard) that becoming a reader of her work is its own defining experience. We rush and try not to rush through her short bursts of strong-minded lyricism. *This is good,* the greedy reader says to herself. *And this. And this.*

FROZEN LOOKS
A GIRL'S LIFE

EVE'S HOLLYWOOD

EVE BABITZ

THE PAST IS ENTERED THROUGH CREAKING IRON GATES
laced with fog and the sheer sigh of Joan Fontaine's memory as she begins, "…sometimes I think of Mandalay." So the movie *Rebecca* commences. Hitchcock's lesson always is that nothing is as it seems, the past too teaches that—and the trick is to unravel with one hand and rearrange with the other so that the complicated mechanics of certain stretches of time have their rhythms evened out. But even Hitchcock doesn't tell everything, and at the end of the movie you don't really know if Rebecca was murdered by her husband or if she used him in her own suicide. Hitchcock knows you can't ever know it all, because time keeps shifting the combinations, time releases details at later dates, time can't be bucked by life except for trapped moments in frozen looks.

The gates to my past aren't rusty, creaking, laced with fog. They're the unceremonious whoosh that the sound of the rear door of a bus made as down I stepped, impatient to drown in the hot, open days of my fourteenth summer. Barefooted on the rough rubber steps, I'd jump from the bus and hurry past the old people on the Palisades, scramble down the cool cement steps to the bridge over Pacific Coast Highway, and turn delirious at the sight of the day of heat cooled only by moments frozen into the summer, isolated like prickly cactus standing in the dawn.

In the mornings of that summer I would awaken seriously at 7:30 already afraid that it might be 7:45 or a tragic 8—but it wasn't. My bathing suit lay on the sandy floor right where I'd taken it off the night before and that and my father's old Mexican shirt, 66¢ for the bus, a dime for a snow cone, and a nickel for a frozen Look bar were securely in my purse as out I went. Sometimes my mother would thrust an orange my way before I was halfway down the block, or a fried egg sandwich, but I wasn't hungry much in those days except to hurry up and get to the beach.

The beach from that summer was called Roadside. It was 1958 and a lot of kids from West LA went there—tough kids with knives, razors, tire irons, and lowered cars. No kids from my school or any of the schools nearby went to Roadside, they went to Sorrento where there were never any fights and where most of the kids from Hollywood High, Fairfax, and Beverly spent their summers listening to "Venus" on the radio or playing volleyball. If I had only known about Sorrento, I never would have gone to the beach so passionately, since Sorrento was a dispassionate beach involved mainly in the junior high and high-school ramifications of polite society, sororities, *Seventeen* magazine, football players, and not getting your hair wet.

I found out about Roadside from the cousin of a friend of mine about a week before school let out for summer. Her name was Carol and she wasn't like anyone I'd ever met, though she seemed perfectly suitable as a playmate for fourteen-year-old virgins, us, and she was a few months younger than us too. She could have been one of those perky types with the ponytail and the rolled-up jeans and called "adorable" because she was small and had large blue eyes. But there was something luxuriously corrupt about her even that first day at my friend's house where we were swimming. She complained of pools as she reclined voluptuously on the canvas mattress, making no attempt to hide her total immersion in the sensuality of being alive and wet under a hot sun. She spoke slowly, she drawled in a nasal, rich-girl nonchalance that pools were all right she supposed but the real thing was the ocean, the waves. "What beach do you go to?" my ordinary school friend asked her Beverly Hills cousin.

"Roadside," Carol drawled. "The surf's always better there."

My friend was shocked and amazed by this blatant confession to cheapness (girls only went to Roadside if they were "cheap"). But Carol's decadence was much more elaborate than mere cheapness and it wasn't until a couple of years later that I learned from another friend, Joy, that Carol, that summer when I knew her, was having simultaneous affairs with a concert pianist friend of her parents, a burglar she'd caught in the living room one Saturday, and Joy's brother, who later hung himself in Chicago and whom Carol could never entrap, his death being his final adieu.

But even I could see that Carol's ponytail had something to do with her sense of humor, which was obscure, jaded, and waltzing to a different drummer. And that shocking her cousin with tales of Roadside was giving Carol the same subtle pleasure that some people get behind the wheel of any functioning car. I listened attentively and later made plans to meet her down there when school let out.

Ever since I was little I'd always spent hours in the ocean when I got near it but the best I could do with a wave was dive through or under it before it crashed and got me. Carol taught me to ride the waves in to shore, to await huge fraught-with-peril breakers with giddy dominance so that I could turn my instinctive fear against itself and foam to shore, a beached, elated body ready to pit myself against the waves again and again until I never got crashed to the bottom of the ocean with my chin in the sand from a wave, not knowing which way was up, until I even lost my giddiness and slid out to sea to await the waves enslaved by hypnotic rhythms. I became a gliding sea-mammal. Fierce, arbitrary waves of green tons escaped out the other side of the complicated mechanics of things not being what they seemed so that finally even my instincts altered and what had before been certain death became a toy, greeted calmly with a relaxed look over the top for perhaps a bigger one. Those were the hot open days of summer I awoke desiring so passionately each morning an hour and a half away by bus.

Few kids from Beverly went to Roadside, and the ones that did, like Carol, went for their own reasons and not to hang around with other kids from Beverly, so Carol and I became accomplices at sea and put our towels next to each other on land where we rarely spoke. (Was she recovering from her lovers by befriending fresh me whose only depravity lay in a consuming determination to master the ocean? Did she find my apprenticeship diverting? I never wondered about that then, though questioning motives is a lesson I've finally had to bone up on.)

The real hoods, the serious ones who'd been up the night before fighting with churchkeys and tire irons or knocking up "cheap" girls, spent the days dozing fully clothed or with only their shirts off on blankets adjacent to the wall that encircled the bathrooms. The rest of us, including Carol and me, lay much nearer the water next to the lifeguard stand and wore bathing suits. But there was no set rule, and there was a loose trade around of people who "went in" and people who "hung on the wall."

The "wall" was autographed with the names of most of the hoods who hung on it and the biggest name, five feet across in giant red print, staggered out unevenly spelling PREACHER.

From the first time I went to Roadside the minute school let out, not a day went by that Preacher wasn't mentioned. Rumor had it that he would be getting "out" in July sometime and then, *then* . . . well, you wouldn't have these penny-ante poker games, these half-assed brawls, these opaque silences when plainclothesmen ventured out onto the beach. When Preacher got out things were gonna really get bitchin' . . . "Did you ever hear about the time Preacher dumped a naked girl into the lifeguard station when the chief was there?..."

Carol had only heard about him, which put her in the same boat as me, and she'd listen to the stories spun out extravagantly in his absence with her wide-open blue eyes and her deceitful ponytail drying in the sun.

The day Preacher got there the texture of the beach changed, emanating from the wall with impulses of dangerous craziness. Three lifeguards instead of the usual one were there with frequent visits from the jeeps that patrolled the shore. Is it because lifeguards don't have guns that they needed three? I scooted past the wall trying to be invisible but anxiously fascinated and heard, "Hey, pass that bottle to Preacher." It was 9:15 a.m.

Carol was lying on her stomach when I got down to our part and I fell on my towel, thrown next to her trying to get back to the relaxed hot and open from the dizzy tight and foolhardy of the wall. The sun bleached my bones into driftwood and burnt all from my thoughts but white, and by ten it blazed overhead so unchecked that Carol and I got up simultaneously without speaking and headed west. Great green Pacific gave way to hours of splendid murderous waves for us to emasculate and adapt fiercely to our foaming trails. And then back out for another...the wave and us, to try another combination.

We went to the hot-dog stand at noon and both got our daily rations of snow cones (mine, pineapple—hers, cherry) and frozen Look bars, which we shattered against the counter in their wrappers and ate the splintered pieces which were heaven—nougat so sweet and reluctant and coated with chocolate. Heaven.

On our way back, just as we got to the wall a fight broke out, noisy and violent with people leaping to their feet in order not to be fallen upon or hit accidentally. A young hood was running and right behind him was Preacher, who chased him half a block in the hot sand under the scorching sun until he felled him and dropped on top of him purple with rage. The bystanders clotted to the fight, blocking our view, so I asked someone why and they said the guy had accused Preacher of cheating at cards, which he did, but you're not supposed to say anything about it, everyone knew that. A ghastly slash of pain rose from the center of the mob, from the fight, a high groan of surprise and horror it was, followed by an echoing murmur of disbelief from the crowd. It filtered back to us that Preacher had bitten the guy's ear off, which made my frozen Look suddenly inedible.

The thing was over, the guy was helped to an emergency hospital by some other hoods, Preacher led an awestruck parade back to the wall with blood on his face and someone said the ear was in his pocket. Carol and I, in the crowd farther back, stood with some others unable to move when the arbitrary force cruised by and suddenly stopped, stared at Carol from twenty feet away with the eyes of a mad Dutchman and then began lurching toward her, stopping only to pick up a fistful of money from the deserted poker game. People began backing away from Carol, so singled out, but I got closer, I think it was to see.

"Hey, you snotty Beverly Hills bitch," he snarled, hitting the nail on the head and looking much older than I thought he'd be, and weatherbeaten—someone told me he was twenty, but he looked a ragged thirty. I thought he might try to tear her bathing suit off, but he shook the money at her impassive, demurely lowered eyes and said, "You rich bitches is all whores of Babylon but you ain't gittin' my money, you can bet your sweet baby ass on that." He waited, gathering strength, deadly and crazy.

From her warmly tanned face she languidly opened her expensive blue eyes wide before narrowing them, transforming them into the eyes of an aristocratic animal whose defense lay in some rapid, paralyzing venom which hissed from the pupils and stopped him in his tracks. She stirred her snow cone while she took her time assessing him from his bloody face to his sandy feet to his blood-soaked pocket and then she lowered her eyes, shrugged, and strolled through the space the crowd had opened for her with me floating in back of her, having no wish to stay on after witnessing that crisis of frozen looks.

Years and years later I heard that Preacher was killed—shot in the stomach five times by an irate husband and that his last words had been, "Go ahead, shoot me."

So the gates to my past are the unceremonious whoosh of the bus doors letting me out into the open summer when I began to learn about the complicated mechanics of things not being what they seem so that later I had the feeling that Preacher, like Rebecca, may have committed suicide and that Carol could somehow see past what things seemed into what things were. But what, then, must Carol have been, that fourteen-year-old creature riding waves, silkenly prone in the sun on hot open days, introducing novices like me to the practice of ignoring instinct, of going beyond giddiness, until I could treat certain death like a toy and calmly look over the top for perhaps a bigger one. She seduced me that summer to trails of corrupt and luxurious entertainments of the moment, to Mandalay...at least, that's the way it seems, especially after the way she presented her would-be killer with his own death in the heat of the day when everything stopped in a frozen look.

ONE-LINERS

"Sometimes I feel like my only friend is the city I live in, the City of Angels."
RED HOT CHILI PEPPERS

"Los Angeles is like a beauty parlor at the end of the universe."
EMILY MORTIMER

"It was the fantasy of every *bato* in or out of Chicanada to put on a zoot suit and play the myth *más chucote que la chingada* (more gangster than a motherfucker)."
EL PACHUCO

"You know, you're really nobody in LA unless you live in a house with a really big door."
STEVE MARTIN

"Fresh-flower-bedecked and blue-skied Los Angeles seemed friendly, peaceful, awash with opportunity and a wonderful place to work."
MERLE ARMITAGE

"Those who dismiss ugly Los Angeles will snark at our traffic, overpriced restaurants, and attitude, too."
WENDY GILMARTIN

"Hollywood, despite the smell of patchouli and rattle of revolver fire, seemed to me to be one of the most respectable towns in America."
H. L. MENCKEN

"The great thing about Granada Hills during this period [early 1960s] was that anything that happened in town was the first time it ever happened."
CHEECH MARIN

"This hill had seedy old apartments at the bottom and fancy estates at the top, and classy little Neutra houses all along the middle."
CAROLYN SEE

"Twelve million people and all of them ready to make a break for it if necessary."
MICHAEL CONNELLY

"Our club's general philosophy is the philosophy of LA itself: Achievement is nothing if you don't have the incredible looks to back it up."
CHRIS ERSKINE

"I'm also comfortably asocial—
a hermit in the middle of Los Angeles."
OCTAVIA BUTLER

"It's nice to be in a place where people may not understand where you're coming from, but they respect it and they're willing to be open to it."
VIDYA VOX

"Run it down the line, Sunset and Vine, blew a half a zip by the Hollywood sign."
SNOOP DOGG

"All the vampires walkin' through the Valley/ Move west down Ventura Boulevard/And all the bad boys are standing in the shadow/All the good girls are home with broken hearts/ And I'm free, free fallin'."
TOM PETTY

"I was pretty great in Canada.
Not so much in Los Angeles."
MATTHEW PERRY

"Driving a Bentley to Target—
only in LA does this make sense."
A. M. HOMES

"I basically consider myself street smart . . . unfortunately that street is Rodeo Drive."
CARRIE FISHER

"My parents decided to go back home to Los Angeles [after release from WWII internment camp], but Los Angeles was not a welcoming place."
GEORGE TAKEI

"Vacant, vacuous Hollywood was everything I ever wanted to mold my life into."
ANDY WARHOL

"Latinos are here, they've been here, and they also know that backup is on the way."
W. KAMAU BELL

"If Los Angeles is a woman reclining billboard model with collagen-puffed lips and silicone-inflated breasts, a woman in a magenta convertible with heart-shaped sunglasses and cotton candy hair; if Los Angeles is this woman, then the San Fernando Valley is her teenybopper sister."
FRANCESCA LIA BLOCK

"I've spent my life studying an event that I may not live to see. I thought it would happen before I retired. The Big One."
LUCY JONES

"In Los Angeles versus the San Gabriel Mountains, it is not always clear which side is losing."
JOHN McPHEE

"The last stop before tomorrow."
JANET FITCH

Untitled (from the series *Venice Stories*), courtesy of Anais Jimenez, age 10, and Venice Arts (Art Mentoring & Education Program, 2016)

VENICE SKATE PARK

THROUGH THE EYES OF YOUTH

Dynamic, diverse, a little bit dodgy: Dogtown. Now used to sell everything from coffee to real estate, the Dogtown name continues to convey the cool it acquired in the 1970s when the area emerged as the birthplace of Southern California's skateboard culture, even as today's Westside tech boom and gentrification bring changes to the beachside Venice neighborhood.

It was in this atmosphere of reflection and transformation that Venice Arts embarked on a yearlong storytelling project with young people who participate in our Art Mentoring & Education Program. Since its founding in 1993, Venice Arts has taught thousands of low-income youth how to use photography and filmmaking to explore the world around them, and to tell personal and community stories through visual media. The Skate Park and the Venice Boardwalk are frequent draws for field shoots, allowing students to explore these community landmarks as they learn to frame compelling compositions, use light and color artistically, stop or blur motion, and capture street portraits—all tools that can enrich photography as an expressive medium. These images from the Skate Park, taken by young people ages ten to eighteen, record the living legacy of Dogtown, part of the vivid tapestry that makes Venice unique.

—Elysa Voshell/Venice Arts

Untitled (Venice Skate Park), courtesy of Jimmy Papik, age 13, and Venice Arts (Summer Media Arts Camp, 2011)

Untitled (from the series *Venice Stories*), courtesy of Paula Contreras, age 11, and Venice Arts (Art Mentoring & Education Program, 2016)

Untitled (*Venice Stories*), courtesy of Niobe Huezo, age 13, and Venice Arts (Art Mentoring & Education Program, 2016)

Untitled (*Venice Stories*), courtesy of Lenny Perez, age 17, and Venice Arts (Summer Media Arts Camp, 2014)

Untitled (*Venice Stories*), courtesy of Lenny Perez, age 17, and Venice Arts (Summer Media Arts Camp, 2014)

Untitled (Venice Skate Park), courtesy of Karla Tamayo, age 17, and Venice Arts (Art Mentoring & Education Program, 2014)

Untitled (*Venice Stories*), courtesy of Katherine Ramirez, age 11, and Venice Arts (Art Mentoring & Education Program, 2016)

This is a transcript from a recording of broadcaster/spoken-word artist Vin Scully's call of the ninth inning of Los Angeles Dodgers pitcher Sandy Koufax's perfect game on September 9, 1965, against the Chicago Cubs. The recording was made and distributed as a souvenir phonograph record sold at the stadium by the Dodgers. Vin Scully called nearly ten thousand games for the Dodgers. He began with the team while they were in Brooklyn, but by 2016 when he retired, his voice had come to mean LA to many Angelenos. LA has an abundance of summer sounds to lift the spirit: the hypnotic surf, the jingling bells of the *paletero* as the ice cream man makes his rounds, the pulsating rainbird sprinkler (a sound-memory so potent for some, there are audios shared on YouTube). But millions of Angelenos have only to turn on the game on the car radio or settle in and take a first sip of beer at Dodger Stadium to hear Mr. Scully in their minds. His call that day, like all his other calls, was composed as the action unfolded.

CALL OF HISTORY
A RADIO MOMENT

THE PERFECT GAME

VIN SCULLY

"THREE TIMES IN HIS SENSATIONAL CAREER HAS SANDY
Koufax walked out to the mound to pitch a fateful ninth where he turned in a
no-hitter. But tonight, September the ninth, nineteen hundred and sixty-five,
he made the toughest walk of his career, I'm sure, because through eight in-
nings he has pitched a perfect game.

"He has struck out eleven, he has retired twenty-four consecutive batters,
and the first man he will look at is catcher Chris Krug, big right-hand hit-
ter—flied to second, grounded to short.

"Dick Tracewski is now at second base and Koufax ready and delivers:
curveball for a strike. O and one the count to Chris Krug. Out on deck to
pinch-hit is one of the men we mentioned earlier as a possible, Joey Amalfitano. Here's the strike-one pitch to Krug: fastball—swung on and missed,
strike two.

"And you can almost *taste* the pressure now. Koufax lifted his cap, ran his
fingers through his black hair, then pulled the cap back down, fussing at the
bill. Krug must feel it too as he backs out, heaves a sigh, took off his helmet,
put it back on, and steps back up to the plate.

"Tracewski is over to his right to fill up the middle; Kennedy is deep to
guard the line. The strike-two pitch on the way: fastball—outside, ball one.

"Krug started to go after it and held up and Torborg held the ball high in
the air trying to convince Vargo, but Eddie said 'No sir.' One and two the
count to Chris Krug.

"It is nine-forty-one p.m. on September the ninth. The one-two pitch on the way: curveball—tapped foul off to the left of the plate.

"The Dodgers defensively in this spine-tingling moment: Sandy Koufax and Jeff Torborg. The boys who will try and stop anything hit their way: Wes Parker, Dick Tracewski, Maury Wills, and John Kennedy; the outfield of Lou Johnson, Willie Davis, and Ron Fairly.

"And there's twenty-nine thousand people in the ballpark and a million butterflies. Twenty-nine thousand, one hundred and thirty-nine paid.

"Koufax into his windup and the one-two pitch: fastball—fouled back out of play.

"In the Dodger dugout Al Ferrara gets up and walks down near the runway, and it begins to get tough to be a teammate and sit in the dugout and have to watch.

"Sandy back of the rubber, now toes it. All the boys in the bullpen straining to get a better look as they look through the wire fence in left field. One and two the count to Chris Krug. Koufax, feet together, now to his windup and the one-two pitch: fastball—outside, ball two.

"A lot of people in the ballpark now are starting to see the pitches with their hearts. The pitch was outside, Torborg tried to pull it over the plate but Vargo, an experienced umpire, wouldn't go for it. Two and two the count to Chris Krug.

"Sandy reading signs, into his windup, two-two pitch: fastball—got him swingin'! Sandy Koufax has struck out twelve. He is two outs away from a perfect game.

"Here is Joe Amalfitano to pinch-hit for Don Kessinger. Amalfitano is from Southern California, from San Pedro. He was an original bonus boy with the Giants. Joey's been around, and as we mentioned earlier, he has helped to beat the Dodgers twice, and on deck is Harvey Kuenn.

"Kennedy is tight to the bag at third, the fastball—a strike. O and one with one out in the ninth inning, one to nothing, Dodgers.

"Sandy reading, into his windup and the strike-one pitch: curveball—tapped foul, O and two. And Amalfitano walks away and shakes himself a little bit, and swings the bat. And Koufax with a new ball, takes a hitch at his belt and walks behind the mound.

"I would think that the mound at Dodger Stadium right now is the loneliest place in the world.

"Sandy fussing, looks in to get his sign, O and two to Amalfitano. The strike-two pitch to Joe: fastball—swung on and missed, strike three!

"He is one out away from the promised land, and Harvey Kuenn is comin' up.

"So Harvey Kuenn is batting for Bob Hendley. The time on the scoreboard is nine-forty-four. The date, September the ninth, nineteen sixty-five, and Koufax working on veteran Harvey Kuenn.

"Sandy into his windup and the pitch, a fastball—for a strike! He has struck out, by the way, five consecutive batters, and that's gone unnoticed. Sandy ready and the strike-one pitch—very high, and he lost his hat. He really forced that one. That's only the second time tonight where I have had the feeling that Sandy threw instead of pitched, trying to get that little extra, and that time he tried so hard his hat fell off. He took an extremely long stride to the plate and Torborg had to go up to get it.

"One and one to Harvey Kuenn. Now he's ready: fastball—high, ball two. You can't blame a man for pushing just a little bit now. Sandy backs off, mops his forehead, runs his left index finger along his forehead, dries it off on his left pants leg. All the while Kuenn just waiting. Now Sandy looks in. Into his windup and the two-one pitch to Kuenn—swung on and missed, strike two!

"It is nine-forty-six p.m.

"Two and two to Harvey Kuenn, one strike away.

"Sandy into his windup, here's the pitch—swung on and missed, a perfect game!

(Thirty-eight seconds of cheering.)

"On the scoreboard in right field it is nine-forty-six p.m. in the City of the Angels, Los Angeles, California. And a crowd of twenty-nine thousand, one hundred thirty-nine just sitting in to see the only pitcher in baseball history to hurl four no-hit, no-run games. He has done it four straight years, and now he caps it: On his fourth no-hitter he made it a perfect game.

"And Sandy Koufax, whose name will always remind you of strikeouts, did it with a flurry. He struck out the last six consecutive batters. So when he wrote his name in capital letters in the record books, that "K" stands out even more than the 'O-U-F-A-X.' "

There are campfire stories and bar stories, and in LA there is the fine art of stuck-in-traffic tale spinning. Dave and Eddie, whose ballad this is, are direct descendants of Bunyon and Babe, except that they both talk. We haven't met Dan Bern, but we picture him as a singing, songwriting guy who hangs out with Cheech Marin and "the Dude" Lebowski. At any rate, he's made the perfect ode to attitude.

THE BALLAD OF DAVE AND EDDIE

DAN BERN

dave and eddie
were at venice beach
playing their guitars
they played for 2 hours
and made 6 dollars
and 37 cents
in change
then they got in dave's car
and headed back to hollywood.
they sat in traffic
it was slow
they took the 405
and then the 10
and then la brea
it took over an hour
to get home.
"jeez," said eddie,
"they need another freeway
in this town."
"yeah," said dave,
"from, like venice beach
to around hollywood and vine."

"yeah," said eddie,
"and with an exit at
la brea and willoughby."
"yeah," said dave,
"and it would hit the
10 and the 405 near the beach
and then rip right through to hollywood."
"yeah," said eddie, "and it
would have an exit by
the beverly center, and
another one on melrose."
"where on melrose?" said dave.
"oh, maybe around fairfax," said eddie.
"yeah," said dave, "near farmers market."
"yeah," said eddie.
it began informally
on weekends and in their
spare time.
dave visited the
hardware store for poles
and wire and steel rods, and
eddie bought several bags of cement powder
at the ready-mix plant.
dave had a friend with a truck
and they started work a
few days later,
pouring their first patch of concrete
near venice boulevard, a
few blocks from the beach.
people stopped to watch. "what're
you guys doing?" one guy asked.
"building a freeway to hollywood,"
said dave, as eddie
pounded a steel girder into place.
"cool," the guy said,
"that's totally excellent."

as work on the freeway progressed,

dave and eddie's
enthusiasm increased.
dave cut back
his hours at the cassette-
copying place,
and eddie arranged to
have thursday and friday
afternoons off at the
guitar center.
"do you think we should
tell the city about this?"
asked dave one day while
they assembled an overpass above sepulveda.
"let's wait," said eddie.
"if it's all done,
they can't really say no."

months passed. strain began
to show on dave and eddie.
they had a big argument
about where to put an
off-ramp near
century city. dave wanted it on
avenue of the stars
a few blocks from santa monica boulevard.
eddie preferred
a bit south
in rancho park, adjacent
to 20th-century fox.
they didn't speak for
two days, and work was
suspended. finally, they
compromised and put it on pico,
further west. "right by
mccabe's guitar shop," said eddie.
"that'll be great."
then there was the matter of the freeway's name.
dave wanted it to be called

the dave, and eddie wanted
it to be called the eddie.
at last they settled
on the dave and eddie
memorial freeway. they thought
"memorial" had an official, freeway-ish
ring to it.

one thursday in late january,
they laid the last section of
concrete. it was the off-ramp onto
franklin and gower, just a few steps from
the corner of hollywood and vine.
"that about wraps it up," said eddie
as the sludge oozed
onto the ground. "voila."
it was 13 months since
they had begun the project.
"dude," said dave.
"that was something."
they got a 12-pack
of pabst blue ribbon
at ralph's and
went over to dave's
to celebrate the completion
of the dave and eddie
memorial freeway.
they drank all the
beer, then went out
and rode the freeway
clear to venice and back,
several times.
without traffic it took exactly
12 minutes round-trip.
"totally excellent," said dave. "and those green
signs we made
are gnarly."

the next day they
opened up the freeway
and the first cars
started rolling on around
eight-fifteen.
dave and eddie stood on the shoulder
and watched.
everyone gave them
the thumbs-up sign.
"looks great!" people shouted.
"excellent job!" "you guys are
all right!"

the next day was friday.
dave got a phone call.
it was a mrs. goldfarb
from the mayor's office.
"we need to talk to you,"
she said. dave said he would
go downtown.

in the mayor's office
mrs. goldfarb peered at him sternly.
"are you the fellow who
built the new freeway?" she demanded.
"yeah," said dave. "me and
my friend eddie."
"you should have asked first,"
said mrs. goldfarb.
"yes, ma'am," said dave.
"well, it's water under the dam,"
said mrs. goldfarb, shuffling
some papers. "the city,
under the auspices of the state,
is prepared to make you an offer
on your freeway."
"you mean," said dave,
"you want to buy it?"

"of course," said mrs. goldfarb,
"you weren't thinking of
keeping it?"
"kind of," said dave. "nonsense," said mrs. goldfarb,
"i'll need a signature, and
we will pay you three million dollars."
"wow," said dave. "that's totally a lot.
can it still be called the
dave and eddie memorial freeway?"
"certainly not," said mrs. goldfarb.
"the state assigns a number
to every freeway. yours has
been designated freeway number 313."
"what if it got called the dave and eddie,"
said dave, "and we got
two million?"
"i'm sorry," said mrs. goldfarb, snapping
shut a notebook and placing
a piece of paper in front
of him to sign.
"it's quite impossible. it will
be the 313."
"in that case,"
said dave, "i won't sign it."
"if you don't," said mrs. goldfarb,
"we will seize the freeway
under territorial zoning act
number 67H
paragraph 5."
"well," said dave.
he signed the paper
and mrs. goldfarb gave
him a check for
three million dollars.

he drove up the 101,
switched over to the 313,
and got off at

fairfax and melrose.
"hey eddie," said dave,
walking into the guitar center.
"i had to sell the freeway."
"what?" eddie croaked.
"how could you sell the freeway?"
"i don't know," said dave.
"i went downtown and everything was real confusing,
and the next thing i knew, it was gone."
"that's so uncool," said eddie, "i can't believe it."
"it was weird," said dave,
"it just sort of happened. we
got three million for it."
"whoa," said eddie. "that's a lot, huh?"
"yeah," said dave. "i'll go cash it
and bring you
a million and a half."
"wait a second," said eddie.
"i spent 600 bucks
to build it. you
only spent, like, 300."
"yeah," said dave. "so?"
"so, like, i invested two times
what you did. i should
get two million."
"bullshit," said dave.
"we split it in half."
"all right," said eddie,
"but you still owe me 300."
"fine," said dave. "and i want
my amplifier back."
"you can have that
piece of shit," said eddie.

the 313 became
very popular as people
sought to decrease their
travel time from hollywood

THE BALLAD OF DAVE AND EDDIE

to venice. to dave and
eddie's delight, the name "313"
never caught on and people
said, "come north on
the 405 and then take
the dave and eddie
until you hit
beverly center."

dave and eddie
still went to
venice beach every sunday
and played their guitars.
one day they got
over thirteen dollars
in just over an hour
and a half.
"wow," said dave.
"we're getting good."
"yeah," said eddie. "maybe
we should make a record."

they took their guitars
and got into dave's car
and headed toward hollywood.
there was so much traffic
on the dave and eddie
that dave and eddie
took the 405 and the
10 and la brea instead.

PHOTO BY ROBERT LANDAU

The Valles, married co-authors, combined their voices and experiences as journalists, academic researchers, and cooks to create a unique cookbook-memoir called *Recipe of Memory*. The core of their book is a treasury of nineteenth- and early-twentieth-century recipes, and it's rich with an expansive sense of place as experienced and remembered through eating and drinking. That's because the Valles created a chain of story-recipes linking the generations of family from their homes in 1880s Guadalajara and Jalisco to 1980s Los Angeles. We eat squab and saffron-cinnamon rice in the lost LA neighborhood of *Canta Ranas* (Singing Frogs). With the mule drivers at the Inn of San Felipe in Guadalajara, we're served *Coles Endiablados* (Deviled Cabbage) and *Sopa de Garbanzo*. In Jalisco, we stop for convent cooking *Leche de Camote Morado y Almendra* (Sweet Potato and Almond Pudding) and hide from bandits but also feast on sardines with poblanos. Settling down in southeast LA County, we marvel at ancient wisdom at work in a suburban backyard.

CHILDREN OF MAYAGUEL

HARVEST

RECIPE OF MEMORY: FIVE GENERATIONS OF MEXICAN CUISINE

VICTOR M. VALLE and MARY LAU VALLE

NOT ALL THE RECIPES DELFINA BROUGHT WITH HER FROM Mexico were written in cookbooks. She scribbled some on loose sheets of paper she dated May 23, 1908, about a year before she married. One such recipe stands out. It was titled *Lomo en Frío con Pulque* (Cold Roast Beef in a Pulque Sauce). *Pulque*, the fermented juice of the agave cactus, commonly known as a century plant, comes to our time right out of Jalisco's pre-Hispanic past. I found it intriguing, but without a supply of *pulque* I assumed the recipe would have to go untested. That's about as far as my curiosity went, at least until my uncle Teófilo called me up on the telephone one May morning in 1982 to show me how the past hides in the present, until summoned forth in recollection.

Teófilo, my Uncle Julio's younger brother, had promised a few months before that he'd show me how to make *pulque* the next time he cracked one of the *magueyes* growing like a huge forbidding pineapple bush in his backyard in La Mirada, a placid Southern California suburb a few miles north of Orange County. For years, I heard my relatives talk about *pulque* with either disgust or yearning, but I didn't really expect Teófilo to show me what all the fuss was about. Still, I was curious enough to find out. And anyway, I thought it might make an interesting feature for the *Los Angeles Times*, where I worked in one of the paper's suburban sections.

I got to his house at about 9 a.m., the time he planned to "crack" the *maguey.* We walked into his patio, where Teófilo showed me his tools, which lay somewhere under the mountains of junk he sold at swap meets. He slowly slid boxes of dusty jars as he struggled to rearrange the antlered aluminum of broken lawn furniture. His eyes, now fading to gray, carefully followed his hands in the triangular shadows created by the *chayote* vine. Rising from the patio's dirt floor, its heavy net of lime leaves camouflaged his garage and clung to his kitchen window. Finally, he straightened himself. In his hands he held a small half-moon saw and large, spoonlike blade for reaching and piercing the *maguey's* white membranous skull.

He then approached the near-tree-size *maguey.* It filled a whole corner of his backyard like some beast bristling with black thorns. He carefully lodged boards between its blue-gray leaves, making a ladder to climb between the small black shark's teeth that gird each leaf, then reached down to the *mezontle,* the boulder-shaped mass of stored juices, and cut the first leaf.

"Cut only a few," he said, "to save *aguamiel,*" the honey-sweet sap the *maguey* "cries" after being wounded. "This is *jiote,*" he added, a spike rising from the *mezontle's* core. This shaft of unfurled leaves grows three houses high before it blossoms bitter, sulfurous flowers that announce the *maguey's* death. He sawed it off at the base, carved a small pocket to fibrous whiteness, a shade which the Aztecs compared to the full moon. Next he filled the cavity with the shavings, and covered it with a smooth round stone to keep insects from fouling the brew. He'd return the next morning to start the bleeding, first ladling out the *aguamiel* that had collected overnight, then carefully scraping away the thin membrane the plant had woven to heal itself. He'd repeat the routine twice a day, making sure the wound stayed fresh, initially extracting *aguamiel* by the pint, and then, after several weeks, by the half gallon.

Teófilo reminded me just how different two brothers can be. At age eight, my uncle Julio was sent to San Pedro Tlaquepaque to begin his schooling with Catalina. Julio so thoroughly adopted city ways that it would be impossible for me to imagine him, years later, at a beach picnic in anything but a tailored suit, tie, and gray fedora. Teófilo stayed behind on the family hacienda in Jalisco, learning the region's indigenous plant lore, waiting several years before following his brothers to Los Angeles. He died in 1986 at age eighty-seven. Everything about his appearance marked him as a descendant of Jalisco's Spanish settlers, but everything he taught me about *magueyes* that morning came from its indigenous inhabitants.

He told me that no part of the *maguey*—its leaves, juices, flowers, roots, and thorns—is wasted. *Pulque,* a syrupy wine, is fermented from the *maguey's* cinnamon-colored juices. The ancient Mexicans also concentrated the unfermented mead into candy; honey was made from its pollen-rich flowers; its large, tuberlike roots were roasted and chewed; and its long thorns became sewing needles. Today, whole *maguey* leaves are still placed in underground barbeque pits. The hot embers make these leaves release their sweet cactus flavor into linen bags holding joints of goat, pork, or beef flavored with chiles and spices. And a tough, parchmentlike material removed from inside the leaf is used for wrapping and steaming pieces of lamb or kid in a delicacy called *mixiotes.*

Anthropologists credit the *maguey* as the unsung lifesaver of Mesoamerican agriculture. *Aguamiel* and *pulque* provided reliable alternatives to water for the peasants during the dry season when shortages of drinking water made work in the fields impossible. Just as importantly, *aguamiel* and *pulque* are foods.

A bit more than six ounces of *pulque,* or two hundred grams, provides thirteen percent of the US recommended daily allowance for thiamine, four percent of riboflavin, and five percent of niacin. The same serving is also high in calcium, exceeding the recommended daily allowance of one milligram, and contains twenty percent of the recommended allowance for vitamin C and four percent of the allowance for iron. Compared to 200 grams of orange juice, pulque is slightly higher in B vitamins and iron, moderately higher in phosphorus and potassium, but lower in vitamin C.

Due to natural organisms living within the *maguey,* fermentation is already under way when the juice is extracted, turning *aguamiel* into *pulque* within twenty-four hours. *Pulque* can reach an alcohol content ranging between eight to ten percent within eighteen days of aging, which explains why *pulque* drinking in pre-Columbian times was strictly regulated. Most people drank *aguamiel* the way we drink milk today. *Pulque* was reserved for the Aztec priests and warriors as a ceremonial intoxicant. The elderly also were permitted to indulge, as long as they did so in the privacy of their homes. But apparently, *pulque* drinking occasionally led to excess, usually when the elderly took their drunkenness into the streets and marketplaces. So the Aztecs devised a ruthlessly efficient way of handling their elderly inebriates—they simply carved out the aged offender's heart on the sacrificial stone.

Still, the ancient Mexicans venerated the *maguey* for its life-sustaining and intoxicating virtues. *Pulque*, the Aztecs believed, was the milk of Mayaguel, the Goddess of One Hundred Breasts who ruled the heaven of drowned children and mothers who died in childbirth. In the Aztec codices, or picture books, she is depicted as a large *maguey* with several breasts from which drowned children suckle in the shade of her leaves. Teófilo, however, didn't have to die to taste the tree of the afterlife.

"I was eleven when I knew *pulque*," Teófilo said the day he taught me to tap his *maguey*. "Hell! Once my uncle Nacho told me, 'You are too poor. I'll give you some tools because the *magueyes* are going bad, shooting up their spikes. Crack *magueyes* and sell *pulque*.' Nacho gave me faculties to do this.

"Over in the big pasture, there must have been three hundred of them," which had grown into a thorny barrier. "They were mean ones, some tall ones. At least eight liters of *aguamiel* they gave each day. Between my brothers and I and two others, we cracked sixty in one blow. Then seventy more. The biggest ones, the prettiest ones. I would find them sloppy with *aguamiel*. And I, sucking *magueyes*, drinking four liters a day," he recounted. "It tasted like *panocha* [raw sugar] with cinnamon, delicious."

He continued extracting *aguamiel* and brewing *pulque*. He boasted of drinking more than a quart of *pulque* each day that summer. He would dilute it with some previously boiled water and loads of crushed ice, and then flavor it with finely diced oranges, onions, and ground, toasted *chile piquín*, or with finely diced pineapple or the plump, yellow, pink-fleshed *guayabas* from his yard. He'd tell me it made his blood strong. But I think he loved *pulque* because of all the attention it brought him.

Each afternoon during that summer, young and mature men, mostly old work mates from Jalisco thirsty for a taste of home, drove up to Teófilo's house for a drink. Or else it was their wives or sisters who came with empty plastic milk containers. They wanted to get away from kids or a sweltering kitchen and sip something cool under the tree in Teófilo's front yard. They'd pay him a nominal fee for his trouble. The transaction, of course, was illegal, but it allowed them to indulge in a few icy glassfuls of *pulque*, which they would sip while sitting on old lawn furniture, each remembering the shade of other trees, of other childhoods. Yet these immigrants, the children of Mayaguel, did not just thirst for memories, but also for a way to honor and preserve them.

But they themselves were too busy working, and their lives too unsettled, to wait a decade for their own *magueyes* to mature. Only someone from another century, with time on his hands, like Teófilo, could dedicate himself to their memories. So they drank as long as the *pulque* lasted, relishing the flavors of conversation and of childhood.

LOMO EN FRÍO CON PULQUE
COLD ROAST BEEF IN A PULQUE SAUCE

SERVES 5 TO 6

Canned pasteurized *pulque* can be purchased in border towns like Tijuana or Juarez. If that's too far to drive, then use a Pilsen-type beer instead.

3½ pounds top round roast or any quality lean beef roast
2 cups pulque, *or a Pilsen-type beer*
3 (1-inch) cinnamon sticks
3 bay leaves
1 teaspoon whole black peppercorns
½ cup chopped white onion
1 cup finely diced tomatoes
6 whole cloves
3 teaspoons salt
2 teaspoons olive oil
½ white onion, sliced into ⅛-inch rings
1 head butter or romaine lettuce, washed and drained
2 tablespoons chopped Spanish capers
¼ cup whole Spanish green olives
7 yellow pickled chiles

PREPARATION

On the day before cooking, place the roast in a deep roasting pan. In a medium bowl, mix *pulque*, cinnamon, bay leaves, peppercorns, chopped onion, tomatoes, cloves, and salt. Rub the spices and *pulque* into the meat. Cover and marinate overnight in the refrigerator.

Preheat oven to 350 degrees. Cook roast for 1½ hours. The meat should be slightly pink. Separate the roast from the pan juices and allow it to cool, setting aside the meat juices.

Heat the olive oil in a large skillet over a medium flame. Sauté the onion rings, then add ¾ cup of strained meat juices and sauté for 2 minutes.

Place the roast on a large cutting board and cut into thin ⅛-inch slices and place on a platter lined with lettuce leaves. Pour the warm sautéed onion sauce over the meat. Decorate with capers, olives, and chiles.

There are moments in fiction when a character and her setting are revealed at memorable points in their separate histories—so their story has magical texture. Cecil Castellucci's novel *Beige* wittily sketches the experience of one teenager marooned for the summer in LA in the early '90s. In the process she tells us much about the special appeal of the city for Canadians and vice versa. Her teen protagonist, Katy, self-consciously a model of her national stereotype, finds herself on the edges of the punk rock world when hardcore had waned but a handful of LA bands had mainstream success. She's alternately polite, appalled, incredulous, and embarrassed as she moves between a Silver Lake apartment complex's pool area, a teen-band rehearsal space, and Guitar Center, never once getting to the beach. But (spoiler alert) things come together for her at the Sunset Junction Street Fair.

SUMMER SUCKS
STRANDED IN SILVER LAKE

BEIGE

CECIL CASTELLUCCI

LOS ANGELES

The first thing I notice as the plane lands at LAX is that it is cloudy and pouring rain. So much for the myth that it's always sunny in Los Angeles.

Never mind. The weather matches my mood, though on the outside I am all clear skies and sunshine. I *smile*. Even though I have to wear an embarrassing Air Canada Unaccompanied Minor baseball hat and a big lanyard around my neck holding a card with my name and address written on it like I'm a six-year-old who might get lost on a school field trip. Even though as I get off the airplane, I am escorted to baggage claim by an overly perky and way-too-in-my-business flight attendant named Candy.

I wish she could just break the rules. I wish she could just leave me alone to face the embarrassment that is my father.

"The Rat will pick you up at the airport, Katy," Mom said when I left Montreal, and I almost thought I heard her say under her breath, *"J'espère."*

I hope.

"Do you see him?" Candy asks, smiling at me. Big teeth. I'm glad to see there is a sesame seed stuck in one of them. I wish a cavity on her while I smile sweetly.

My eyes scan the baggage claim area. Any number of the men standing around looking eagerly like they are waiting for someone could be The Rat. I almost don't want to find him, like maybe it would be best for everyone involved if he just forgot to show up. From what I know of him, that could

120

happen. That's not even stretching my imagination. If he didn't show up, I could shrug, say I tried, and go to Peru.

I size up this one older guy. He's distinguished-looking, wearing a button-down green shirt and khaki pants. The man looks like he's wearing his Sunday-best-trying-to-impress, like a cleaned-up version of the last picture I have of The Rat. He could be The Rat. Sort of. If I squint. I am almost relieved. I could maybe hang with this guy for two and a half weeks. Maybe. I start to make my way toward him. But then someone else catches my eye and my heart sinks.

"Yeah," I say to Candy. "I see him."

Everybody sees him.

The Rat is six feet five inches tall and wears a tiny cowboy hat on his head. He's got a rolled-up cigarette (I hope not a joint) hanging out of his mouth, and his skinny sleeve-tattooed arms poke out of his once black, now faded gray T-shirt that says NOSTRA DUMB ASS. He is scruffy, greasy, unshaven, and probably unwashed. His pegged jeans are dingy and look like he wears them every single day.

My father, Beau Ratner, punk name The Rat, looks just like a bum.

As soon as he sees me, he stands up on the edge of the baggage claim belt, throws his hands in the air, waves them around, and yells, "Hellloooooooooooo, Katy!" [. . .]

An alarm signals and the suitcases start to spit out onto the spinning conveyor belt. The Rat jumps off the belt and runs toward me and swoops me up into a back-cracking bear hug.

"Look at you! Look at you! You're huge!" he says. "I can't believe how much you've grown. I mean, of course I've seen the pictures. But now you're here! In the flesh!"

The Rat is all bending and hugging me, and I am as stiff as a board. I can't relax. It doesn't feel natural. I want to remind him that he's not anything to me that I would call Dad. He hasn't even come to visit me in Canada since I was seven years old. I want to remind him that to me he is just e-mails, phone calls, some letters, and a bunch of awkward presents.

"Your guitar will probably be with the oversized luggage," he says. "I'll go pick it up while you watch for your bags."

He rushes over to get the guitar that I didn't ask for and didn't need. I definitely didn't want to bring it with me to California. But Mom insisted. "Music is his life," she always says with a smile that looks like a secret.

"His life," I remind her. "Not mine."

The Rat has been the drummer in about a million bands, but he's best known for being in a band called Suck.

I might not *know* music, I might not like music, but everyone with half a brain knows the band Suck. They were never famous. They were more like infamous. Infamously un-famous. Infamously messed up. Infamously the greatest band that never made it.

I have tried to listen to the seven-inch vinyls my mom swears are classics. I have tried to listen to the CD reissue of their out-of-print first (and only) full-length record. Nails on a chalkboard sound more pleasing.

But no matter how much I protested, the guitar, a purple acoustic/electric Daisy Rock guitar, a present for my thirteenth birthday, had to come with me to California.

I have taken it out of its case exactly three times. Mom always says you should try something truly and completely before you give it up. She knows of what she speaks, though perhaps in her day she has taken that idea a bit too far. But it's a good point. It's following an academic line of inquiry.

I, myself, discovered that I feel about the guitar the way I feel about eating eel. I knew I wouldn't like it as soon as I set my eyes on it. Trying it didn't change anything.

It didn't matter. She wouldn't budge. She insisted. So there was no getting out of taking the guitar along for the miserable ride.

With the help of a stranger, I struggle to pull my bags off the moving belt, and The Rat returns with my guitar in his hands, pumping it over his head like it's a trophy.

"It's like a crazy exciting time now," he says. "Sam is really back. Really ready to start Suck again. And this time I think it's going to take!"

We push the bags over to his beat-up hatchback. It sports stickers on the bumper: DESTROY ALL MUSIC and KILL RADIO and KXLU and SEA LEVEL RECORDS and KCRW and AMOEBA RECORDS and INDIE 103, and we have a hard time shoving my bags and the guitar into the backseat because the trunk is filled up with The Rat's drum kit.

"It's not my full drum kit. It's my emergency drum kit," he says. "You know, in case I need to get to some gig or rehearsal last minute."

Normal people keep spare tires and emergency roadside kits in their trunk, but The Rat needs to be able to cover rock emergencies.

I nearly have a heart attack when the car starts because the radio comes on at about one bagazillion decibels. The Rat must have serious ear damage or, more likely, severe brain damage.

"Let me turn down the music, so we can talk," he says, leaning over. "First of all, I think you should call me Beau, because *The Rat* doesn't sound right for us and *Dad* feels kind of weird. Unless you want to call me Dad? Or The Rat? Or you know what? How about I'll leave it up to you? What do you think?"

As he talks a mile a minute, his hands never stop thumping out a beat on the steering wheel. I don't get a word in edgewise because he just keeps talking and talking and talking, mostly about Suck and their new plans and the old days. Every so often he remembers that I'm in the car and remembers he's excited that I'm here visiting.

I'll just pretend the next two and a half weeks are already over. I'm glad it's a temporary situation. I'll pretend it's a bad dream. That way I'm already back home, with my friends. Living with my mother. Enjoying the rest of my summer.

I try to forget that I am not in Canada today, and that today is Canada Day, our national holiday, July 1.

"This is great," The Rat says, "because I can show you everything. From now on, when I write, you'll be able to picture it all in your head."

He's still babbling away as we walk up the steps to his apartment.

"And see, we're on Sunset Boulevard, so there's plenty for you to do without having a car, 'cause Los Angeles is mostly a car town. You need a car here. Not like in Montreal." [. . .]

ROOTS RADICAL

The Rat and I are sitting outside at Millie's eating breakfast. We don't say much, The Rat and me; we just eat in silence and drink coffee. I am growing to like the tradition, but I don't tell The Rat that. I like that going out for breakfast gets you out into the world. It is easier than cooking at home in the morning.

"That's a nice shirt," The Rat says to the waiter, breaking the silence.

The waiter shakes hands with The Rat.

"Goodwill."

"Good deal," The Rat says. "I like the color and the snap buttons."

The waiter goes off to get us more coffee.

"He's in a great band. They are like insane," The Rat says. "Love their sound."

"His shirt has holes in it."

"So? It still looks good."

If you're homeless, I think.

"Do you want to go thrifting?" The Rat asks. "That could be a fun thing for us to do together."

"No," I say.

"Don't you and your mom go thrifting?"

"Mom and I never shop at Village des Valeurs," I say. "We donate there."

"Ah. Your mom was a good thrifter, back in the day."

It's hard to imagine Mom wearing used clothing. It's so not her style.

Then I remind myself, it's not her style *anymore.*

A bunch of skater kids whiz by, and my eyes follow them. One of the boys is wearing black kneepads, the baggiest black shorts I have ever seen, black elbow pads, a black T-shirt, and a black helmet. In white letters on the back of his helmet it says GARTH SKATER.

The boys pop their boards into their hands, and when the light turns green, they drop them back down and skate across the street in the little square that has a fountain in it.

I watch them as they do their hanging out thing.

The Garth Skater kid…skates up to us. He's kind of hovering by our table.…

I stare at him. He nods at me. I don't nod back.

He leans over and taps The Rat on the shoulder.

"Are you The Rat from Suck?" Garth Skater asks.

"Yeah." The Rat lights up.

"Wow, man. You're like, my hero. I mean, like my drumming hero."

"Well, thanks, man," The Rat says.

"I thought it was you. I've seen you at Millie's before, but I was too scared to talk to you. I mean, you know. I wasn't sure."

"Well, it's me," The Rat says.

"I have every single bootleg of Suck. I also have every single version of every song that any band has ever covered of Suck. I mean, you guys are like *the* Los Angeles band."

"Well, thanks," The Rat says.

"I mean, I'm just so honored to be breathing the same air as The Rat."

"Well, don't hyperventilate. I'm just a guy like you."

"I'm a drummer, too, you know." Garth Skater air drums intensely and bobs his head up and down and bites on his lower lip. I think it's supposed to show his passion, but it just looks kind of dorky. He finishes with a fake flourish and bows. The Rat actually applauds.

"Wow, The Rat!" Garth dorkily punches fists together. Then his skateboard slips from between his knees and rolls away from him.

"Well, see you," The Rat says after Garth as he goes and chases his runaway board. "Oh, and Suck is playing at Sunset Junction. You know. If you're around."

LIVE FAST DIE YOUNG

The Rat finishes his omelet and drains his cup of coffee. Then he readjusts his tiny cowboy hat, lets out a big sigh, and picks up his toolbox from the floor. He jerks his thumb for me to follow him. He settles up the bill, and we head out the door.

"I gotta go to work. You going to be okay on your own?" he asks.

"Yeah." I remind him, "I'm almost fifteen."

"Right, you're a young lady," The Rat says, kind of chuckling to himself. Like he thinks it's funny. It's not.…

I walk down to Sunset Boulevard and explore the neighborhood, by myself. On the way there, I pass that guy I always see walking everywhere in the neighborhood. He's either reading or listening to a little radio or talking on his cell phone. He ignores me when I nod politely to him.

On Sunset there are four cafes, a florist, a cheese shop, a bunch of clothing stores, and a bunch of furniture stores. If I had money, I could spend it really easily. Maybe babysitting for Trixie isn't such an awful idea.

No.

Wait.

It is awful.

My summer job could have been making discoveries relevant to the study of civilization. And now I'll be changing diapers.

One of the clothing stores has all old vintage clothes. I don't want to go in there. The salesgirl seems like she'd laugh at anything I looked at. Besides, it's a bit too funky for me in there. But outside on the sidewalk there is a five-dollar sale rack. That's pretty cheap. I could get a lot of stuff for five dollars. I could just check it out. I pull through the clothes, even though I'm sure there's nothing here I would wear. But there is no harm in looking. I'm holding onto a pale-pink beaded sweater when I look up and I see Leo running toward me. Leo. He's reading an extreme sports magazine. He's going to pass right next to me.

I'm prepared.

I lift my hand up and I say, "Hello!"

He doesn't even slow down. He doesn't even look up. He totally ignores me and just keeps walking.

"Hi!" someone says back. I look over the rack of clothing.

It's that kid with the helmet. I read his name again. Garth Skater.

"You're The Rat's kid, right?" he says. "How are you? That is so cool that you remembered me. I didn't think you'd remember me."

He licks his finger and scores himself a one in the air.

I wasn't even saying hello to him. I then kind of want to remind him that he's wearing a helmet! With his name on it! Who wouldn't remember him?

"What's your name again?" he asks.

I don't want to tell him my name. It's none of his business. But he's looking at me so expectantly. I guess I should say something.

"Beige," I say.

He furrows his brow, like he doesn't understand me.

"Beige," I say a little louder. The name feels strange on my tongue.

"Oh! I get it! It's ironic! 'Cause you're so cool! *Nice.* I like it. Beeeeeeeee-iggggggggge!"

He makes his hand surf the air in front of him as he says it.

"Anyway, see ya," I say, and I walk away. I'll head to the Los Feliz Library. It'll be a cool escape in there. And there are computers. I've decided to go through all the classics they have in the teen section. I'm going to start on the letter zed and go backward. Why start at the beginning? I bet no one ever actually gets to zed. I kind of feel bad for zed. I'll be the girl that loves zed.

"Hey, wait up! Beige!"

I don't turn around at first, because I forget that I told him Beige was my name.

"Yo!" Garth skates up to me.

"Yeah?" I say.

"Wanna hang out sometime?" he says.

He blurts it out. Unsmooth. Is he asking me out? I don't want him to be asking me out. That's not right. Then again it doesn't feel like he's asking me out, like a boy asks out a girl. It feels safe. It feels like he just wants to be friends with me. Maybe he just wants to hang out with me because of The Rat. No one has ever wanted to be friends with me because of that reason. I wonder if he's using me. He doesn't look like a user.

I shrug.

"Okay, great!" he says. "That's wicked! I'm around here all the time 'cause I'm taking drum lessons at the Silverlake Conservatory of Music. Actually I'm late for my lesson. So, you know, cool! I'll see you!"

And then he skates awkwardly away.

What a mess he is! He didn't even ask for my number. He doesn't even know how to get in touch with me. He's the biggest loser I've ever met. Even bigger than me.

And now he thinks my name is *Beige*.

PHOTO BY DARBIE MAR, AGE 17/VENICE ARTS

A bird's-eye view is from above, on high, but not too high. Imagine yourself as a friendly, mind-reading bird. One of those ever-present, all-knowing urbanites— a gull, maybe. A watchful crow. You follow along with Araceli, Héctor Tobar's heroine, as she moves through LA and Southern California. You swoop down and catch her comment to one of the boys she's taking care of, then fly a bit ahead of them to wait on a branch or fence. While you wait and watch, you catch the inner thoughts of this person or that one as they pass through your mind-reading range. Then you fly up and play on the air currents a bit, maybe surfing the downdrafts from the hills, taking in the whole of the basin, sometimes the valleys and the sea. Araceli's on the move again and it's time to hover gently, invisibly, over her shoulder, never invading her space but staying in sync with her all the way. You have other people you could hang with, but she's such a good choice, you linger for days.

THIRTY-NINTH STREET

HEROIC QUEST

THE BARBARIAN NURSERIES

HÉCTOR TOBAR

THEY STEPPED FROM THE BUS TO THE SIDEWALK AND THE door closed behind them with a clank and a hydraulic sigh. Araceli took in the yellowgray heat and the low sun screaming through the soiled screen of the central-city atmosphere. *Goodbye blue skies and sea breezes of Laguna Rancho*, Araceli thought. This was more like the bowl of machine-baked air of her hometown: she had forgotten the feeling of standing in the still and ugly oxygen of a real city. "We walk. That way," Araceli said, pointing south down a long thoroughfare that ran perpendicular to the street the bus had left them on, the four lanes running straight toward a line of distant palm trees that grew shorter until they were toothpicks swallowed up by the haze.

"This doesn't look like the place my grandfather lives," Brandon said.

"Is it close?" Keenan asked.

"*Sí*. Just a few blocks." They stood alone, housekeeper and young charges, on a block where only the bus bench and shelter interrupted the empty sweep of the sidewalk. So strange, Araceli observed, a block without people, just as on Paseo Linda Bonita, but this time in the middle of an aging city with buildings from the previous century. All the storefronts were shuttered and locks as big as oranges dangled from their steel doors, while swarthy men struck poses for the passing motorists from rooftop billboards, their fingers enviously wrapped around light-skinned women and bottles of beer and hard liquor. For a moment Araceli thought that Brandon might be right, that *el viejo* Torres could not live near here. Then again, you never knew in Los Angeles what you might find around the next corner. You could be in the quiet, sunny, and gritty desolation of a block like this at one moment, and find yourself on a tree-lined, shady, and glimmering block of apartments the next. Mexico City was like that too.

Once again, the wheels of the boys' suitcases clack-clacked on the sidewalk as they marched southward. "This doesn't look like where he lives," Brandon repeated, annoying Araceli. "In fact, I'm pretty sure this isn't the place."

"It's just a few blocks," she insisted. In a few minutes she would be free of the care of these two boys and the pressure would be lifted from her temples. Their grandfather would emerge from his door, she would tell him the story of the table and the empty house, and he would make them an early dinner and she would be free of them. They advanced southward, witnessed only by the passing motorists, who were all accelerating on this stretch of relatively open roadway, going too fast to take much note of the caravan of pedestrians headed southward in single file, a boy with rock-star-long hair leading the way, his brow wrinkled skeptically, a smaller child behind him, and a big-boned Mexican woman bringing up the rear and studying the street signs. These were the final minutes before the clock struck five, and the drivers were eager to cover as much ground as possible before the skyline to the north began to empty of clerks, analysts, corporate vice presidents, cafeteria workers, public relations specialists, sales wizards, and assorted other salaried slaves. On this midsummer day, most of these automobiles proceeded with windows sealed and artificial alpine breezes blowing inside, but the air-conditioning was not working inside the Toyota Cressida of Judge Robert Adalian, a jurist at the nearby concrete bunker known as Los Angeles Municipal Traffic Court—Central District. Judge Adalian was driving with the windows open when Araceli, Brandon, and Keenan passed before him at the crosswalk on Thirty-seventh Street and South Broadway, thanks to the rare red light on his drive northward along Broadway, his daily detour of choice to avoid the Harbor Freeway. These pedestrians pushed the button to cross and broke the sequence of the lights, the judge thought as he took in the odd spectacle of a woman who was clearly Mexican with two boys who were clearly not. *It's not their skin tone that gives the boys away, it's their hair and the way they're walking and studying everything around them like tourists. Those boys don't belong here.* Through his open window he caught a snippet of their talk.

"I think we're lost," the taller boy said.

"No seas ridiculo, no estamos lost," the Mexican woman answered, irritated,

and the judge chuckled, because he'd grown up in Hollywood with some Guatemalans and Salvadorans, and the Mexican woman's brief use of Spanglish transported him to that time and place, twenty years ago, when Spanish could still be heard in his old neighborhood, before that final exodus from the old Soviet Union had filled up the neighborhood with so many refugees from the old country (including his future wife) that the city had put up signs around it announcing LITTLE ARMENIA. The light turned green and the judge quickly filed away the Mexican woman and the American boys in the back of his memory, alongside the other unusual event of the afternoon: the sentencing of a onetime sitcom actor whose career had been so brief and distant in time, only the judge recalled it. It had depressed the judge to think that, at forty-four, he was older than his bailiff, his clerk, and his stenographer, older also than the defense attorney and the representative from the city attorney's office. Only the accused surpassed him in age, and when Judge Adalian finally realized that no one in the court was aware of the defendant's contribution to television history, the fifty-two-year-old drunk driving defendant had looked at the judge and raised his eyebrows in an expression of shared generational weariness. "Time passes," the defendant said, and this too struck a chord in the judge's memory, because it wasn't often that the alcoholics who passed through his court imparted any wisdom. The light turned green and the judge glided northward, unaware that in a few weeks' time his memory of crossing paths with the faded actor and the Mexican woman with the two "white" boys on the same ordinary day would win him an appearance on cable television.

Araceli reached the curb on the other side of Broadway and turned right, Brandon now bringing up the rear, because he felt the need to protect his younger brother by walking behind him, lest some monster or Fire-Swallower emerge from one of the shuttered storefronts.

"Don't look at anyone in the eye, Keenan," Brandon said.

"What?"

"This is a dangerous place."

"You can't tell me what to do."

"There might be bad guys inside these buildings," Brandon insisted. "Look at the markings. That's a bad number. Thirteen."

"Really?" Keenan said, and for a moment he saw the world as his brother did, thinking that XIII had to be some warrior code.

Logic told Araceli she was just two blocks away from the address on the back of the old photograph, but now she too was beginning to have serious doubts, given the ominous, spray-painted repetitions of the number 13 on the walls and the sidewalk. She sensed, for the first time, that her naïveté about the city might be leading them to the place where graffiti scribblers and gang members were nurtured under the opaque roof of the smoggy sky, a kind of greenhouse nursery of mannish dysfunction. Now they walked past a large vacant lot, a rectangle filled with knee-high milkweed and trash, which in the glory days of *el abuelo* Torres had been the Lido Broadway movie theater. As a young man *el abuelo* Torres had seen *High School Confidential* screened here, lusted after the curvy starlet Cleo Moore, and been pummeled by a couple of African-American guys who didn't appreciate his comments during a midweek matinee of *Blackboard Jungle.* Juan Torres and his parents were still in the city-to-farm circuit then, forced with a number of other Mexican-American families to live among the blacks. Juan fought the black guys over girls, too. Living here and tasting blood in his mouth had shaped his sense of racial hierarchy, and his ideas about where he fit in the pigmented pyramid of privilege that he understood the United States to be. *As dark as we are, we ain't the bottom.* When he had a glass of sangria or a shot of whiskey too many, the brawling, proud, and prejudiced Johnny Torres of Thirty-ninth Street and the Lido Broadway was resurrected: as during Keenan's sixth birthday party, when he remarked very loudly how fair-skinned and "good-looking" his younger grandson was—"a real white boy, that one"—a remark that led his progressive daughter-in-law to banish him from her home.

If Araceli had not been trailing two children, if she had not been anxious to reach the place that would liberate her from her unwanted role as caretaker of two boys, she might have stopped and taken the time to study the rubble of the Lido Broadway, a half dozen pipes rising from a cracking cement floor like raised hands in a classroom. Time worked more aggressively in the heart of an American city than in a Mexican city, where colonial structures breezed through the centuries without much difficulty. Here, cement, steel, and brick began to surrender after just a decade or two of abandonment. *The people who lived and worked here ran away. But from what?* It was best to keep moving quickly. She spotted a woman pushing a stroller on the next block and a young child walking beside her, two hundred yards away, next to a liquor store with a painted mural of the Virgin of Guadalupe on its side.

Araceli walked toward the store and the Virgin, and soon she and the boys were entering a neighborhood with houses and apartment buildings that were occupied, clapboard structures, mostly, some with iron fences enclosing rosebushes. They saw a woman flinging a carpet against the stairs of a porch that led to a two-story building with four doors. Brandon noted the strange numbers above each entrance—3754¼, 3754½, 3764¾—and was reminded of the fanciful numbered railroad platform from a famous children's book; he wondered if these doors too might be a portal to a secret world. They passed a two-story clapboard with the rusted steel bars of a prison, and both boys wondered if some bad guy was being held inside, but a few doors down, saw an identical structure, with no bars and freshly painted coral-colored walls, an organ pipe cactus rising ten feet high in the garden, alongside a small terra-cotta fountain with running water and a cherub on top. "That's a nice house," Keenan said. *"Muy bonito,"* he added, and Araceli thought, yes, they must be on the right track, because the houses were suddenly getting prettier. But half a block farther along they encountered a square-shaped rooming house whose doors and windows had been boarded up, the plywood rectangles forming the eyes and mouth of a blindfolded and muzzled creature. "I really don't think my grandfather lives around here," Brandon said again, and this time Araceli didn't bother answering him.

Two blocks later they arrived at a street sign announcing Thirty-ninth Street and the final confirmation of Araceli's folly: on this block, where the photograph and the street name on the back had led her, there was a collection of powder-blue duplex bungalows, apartments in a two-story clapboard building surrounded by snowflakes of white paint, and two windowless stucco industrial cubes. The address corresponded to one of the bungalows, which faced the street, with side doors opening to a narrow courtyard. Araceli reached into Maureen's backpack, retrieved the old photograph, and matched the bungalow behind the young *abuelo* Torres to the structure before her: the windows were covered with steel bars now and the old screen door had given way to a fortress shield of perforated steel, but it was the same building. Together, the two images, past and present, were a commentary on the cruelty of time and its passage, and of Araceli's chronological illiteracy, her ignorance of the forces of local history. After a day of walking and bus and train rides she had arrived at her destination, and it was clear that *el abuelo* Torres did not live here, and could not live here, because everything about the place screamed poverty and Latin America, from the wheeled office chair someone had left in the middle of the courtyard amid a pool of cigarette butts to the strains of reggaeton music pulsating from inside one of the bungalows.

"La fregué," Araceli muttered to herself, which caused both boys to look up at her in confusion.

"Is this it?" Brandon said. "Is this the address?"

"Sí. Y aquí no vive tu abuelo."

"No, he doesn't," Brandon said. "His house is in a big apartment complex, with a big lawn in front. It's yellow. And there aren't any ugly buildings like those over there."

"Now what?" asked Keenan.

Behind the security door of the bungalow directly before them, Araceli could hear a second, inner door opening. *"Se le ofrece algo?"* a female voice asked through the perforated steel shield.

Araceli walked to the door and held up the photograph. *"Estoy buscando a este hombre,"* she said. *"Vivía aquí."*

Seeing no danger in a *mexicana* with two young boys, the woman opened the steel door and reached out to take the picture, revealing herself to Araceli as a world-weary woman of about thirty whose smooth skin and long, swept-back eyes appeared to have been carved from soapstone. Her nails were painted pumpkin and her hair seemed oddly stiff and perky, given the circles under her eyes, but those same eyes quickly brightened as she took in the photograph.

"Pero esta foto tiene años y años!" the woman declared, and chuckled after recognizing the black-and-white porch and arriving at the realization that the little shotgun house with the sagging doors and peeling faux linoleum in which she lived had been standing so long, and that once it had been possible to live there without metal barriers to keep out predators: she wouldn't live there now without bars on the windows. She returned the photograph and gave Araceli and the boys the same dismissive look she gave the impossibly earnest young men with narrow ties who visited her earlier in the day searching for the family of Salvadoran Mormons that had once occupied this same bungalow. *"Ni idea,"* the woman said.

Araceli stomped on the wooden porch in frustration. A day on foot, in trains, and buses, from station to station, neighborhood to neighborhood: for this? In the time they had walked from the bus stop the sun had dipped below the buildings on the horizon, the western sky had begun its transformation into the colors of a smoldering hearth. She looked down at the boys and wondered if they would be able to make it all the way back to Paseo Linda Bonita and how much trouble they would become once she told them they would have to start walking again.

The woman at the door sensed Araceli's predicament, which was centered on the presence of the two boys behind her, both of whom seemed to be English speakers. "I think someone I know can help you," she said, switching languages for the benefit of the boys. "*El negro.* He lives right here behind me. Apartment B. I think he's the oldest person who lives here. They say he's been here forever."

A minute or so later Araceli was knocking on the steel door with the B next to it.

"Who the hell is it? What are ya knockin' so loud for, goddamnit!" Behind the perforated steel sheet, an inner door of wood opened, and Araceli saw the silhouette of a large man with thick arms and a slightly curvy posture. "Oh, shit. Didn't know you had the kids with you," the voice said. "What? What you need?"

"I am looking for this person," Araceli said.

"Huh?"

"I am looking for the man in this picture. His name is Torres."

The man opened the door, slowly, and stretched out a weatherworn hand to take the picture, examining it behind his screen. "Whoa! This takes me back!" the man shouted. Now the door opened fully and the man looked down the three steps of his porch to examine the woman who had given him this artifact. He was a bald black man, inexplicably wearing a sweater on this late afternoon in July, and when he fully opened his door the sound of a television baseball announcer filtered out, causing Brandon to stand up on his tiptoes and try to look inside. The man from Apartment B was easily in his seventies, and still tall despite the stoop in his back. The spaces under his eyes were covered with small polyps, and his cheeks with white stubble.

"What are you? His relative? His daughter?"

"No. They are his, how do you say…?"

"He's our grandfather," Keenan offered.

"You know, there's been a lot of people in and out of this place since I moved here."

James "Sweet Hands" Washington had arrived on Thirty-ninth Street as a single man in the middle of the last century, picking out these bungalows because they reminded him of the old shotgun houses in his native Louisiana. The spot at the end of the block occupied by the garment factory had been the site of a car-repair shop back then, and Sweet Hands had worked there for a number of years, dismantling carburetors with the hands dubbed "sweet" first for his exploits on the football field, and later for his exploits with the ladies. Sweet Hands examined the picture, the way the Mexican subject wore his khaki pants with a distinctive mid-1950s swagger, and then the bungalow in the background, and was momentarily transported to that time, when the Southern California sky was dirtier than it was today, and when Sweet Hands himself was a young man recently liberated from Southern strictures. This young man in the photograph looked like he had been liberated too: or maybe he was just feeling what Los Angeles was back then, in that era of hairspray and starched clothes, when the city had a proper stiffness to it, and also a certain glimmer, like the shine of those freshly waxed VS cruisers that rolled along Central Avenue at a parade pace of fifteen miles per hour. Sweet Hands held the picture a long time, and finally let out a short grunt that was his bodily summation of all the emotions this unexpected encounter with the distant past had brought him. "Johnny. That's his name. Johnny something."

"Torres."

"Oh, yeah. Johnny. Johnny Torres. I remember the Torres people." They were one of the first Mexican families to move into these bungalows, way back when Mexico was a novelty Sweet Hands associated with sombreros, donkeys, and dark-eyed beauties with braids and long skirts that reached down to white socks and patent leather shoes. After the Torres people had left—four of them, he seemed to remember, including khaki-pants Johnny here—there hadn't been many other Mexicans around until well after the Watts troubles. They started to show up in large numbers in the years before the Rodney King mess, in fact. It was quite a thing to be able to measure the passing of time by the conflagrations one had seen, by the looting crowds and the fire-makers. Bad times chased away his "people" in all the senses of the word: his relatives, his fellow Louisiana exiles, and most of the other sons of Africa who once lived here. His people had gone off to live in the desert, leaving the place to the Mexicans. Sweet Hands understood, from the way they carried themselves and from the singsong cadences he detected in their speech (without understanding precisely what it was that they were saying), that they came from a verdant place like his own Marion, a place of unrelenting greenness and tangled branches where the rain made songs on the tin roofs. The Mexicans brought with them that slow, boisterous, and tropical feel of rural Louisiana, and he liked having them around, especially since all his relatives had moved out to Lancaster. The few times his daughter and grandchildren came back in their clean and ironed clothes and told him "This place stinks" were enough for him to ask that they not come back—and to resist their entreaties that he move out to the desert. Here on Thirty-ninth Street, Sweet Hands could still take a couple of buses and find the last place in South Los Angeles that served Louisiana buffalo fish, and he might find two or three other old-timers there to talk about baseball and Duke Snider and

Roy Campanella, and watching the Yankees play the Los Angeles Angels in 1961 at the old Wrigley Field, just a short walk away on Forty-second Place. There wasn't any buffalo fish in Lancaster, it was dry as all hell out there, not a place for a man from Louisiana to live. Whereas on certain moist summer mornings the seagulls came to Thirty-ninth Street and circled over the trash cans behind the garment factory, where the taco trucks tossed the tortillas they didn't sell. When Sweet Hands closed his eyes and listened to the caw-caw of the seagulls, he could see the ocean.

"Yeah, I remember this guy," Sweet Hands said finally. "He used to live right there. Where Isabel and her kids live now. Moved out ages and ages ago. I think he moved to the desert. Or to Huntington Park. Used to be that Huntington Park was all the rage. A lot of people from here moved to HP, especially after they opened up that Ford plant...." With that he returned the photograph to Araceli, who looked crestfallen. "Sorry." He gently closed the door and got back to his Dodgers, even as Brandon and Keenan stood up on their tiptoes to get a glimpse of the television inside.

"Now what do we do, Araceli?" Keenan asked as they walked back toward the street. The question echoed in Araceli's mind in Spanish: ¿Y ahora que hacemos? Araceli looked down Thirty-ninth Street and the end of the path she had followed to get to this place. It would be dark by the time they reached the bus stop and she sensed that walking through these neighborhoods at dusk could be worse than putting the boys into foster care, and that the best course of action might be to simply pick up the nearest pay phone and call 911. "Maybe we should go to this Huntington Park place," Brandon offered. "That sounds like the kind of place my grandfather would live...by a park." This absurd suggestion only made Araceli feel more trapped and desperate. *I am the woman who cleans!* She pulled down angrily at her blouse, which had been bunching up on her since they had left the house, then plopped herself down on the edge of the sidewalk. The boys followed, their Velcro-strapped tennis shoes next to her white, scuffed-up nurse's shoes in the gutter.

The unwanted closeness caused the muscles of her legs and back to tense. *Why are you so spoiled and helpless? Why can't you have one nosy aunt or uncle or cousin nearby like all the other children on earth?* She was going to have to make a decision about them. Was $250 stuffed in an envelope every week enough to justify this march across the city? Looking across the street and to her right, she saw a phone booth. If she just picked up the line and called, then maybe she could get the foster care people without summoning the police. *And then I would be free.* Down the block to Araceli's left, a group of squat men and women with round faces gathered around a taco truck, in a chatty cluster before the swing shift began at what she guessed was a garment factory. Behind them she could see a loading dock with a large opening to a vast interior space with low ceilings and a bluish glow, engines groaning and puffing metallically. The boys from the Room of a Thousand Wonders did not know that there was a world of dangerous machines and a city of dark alleys all around them. Having been thrown together with these two boys, in the inescapably intimate situation of being their sole caretaker, Araceli suddenly felt the great distance that separated her life from theirs. *I am a member of the tribe of chemical cleansers, of brooms, of machetes and shovels, and they are the people of pens and keyboards. We are people whose skin bakes in the sun, while they labor and live in fluorescent shadows, covering their skins with protective creams when they venture outside.* Deeper and farther away to the south, beyond the mean city, there were rocky landscapes where men dug tunnels under steel fences, and deserts where children begged for water and asked their fathers if the next ridge was the last one, and cried when the answer was no. Brandon and Keenan did not know of such horrors, but Araceli did, and had survived them, and she wondered how many scars the boys might have after a night or two, or perhaps a week or a month, in foster care, which she imagined to be an anteroom to that dark and dangerous world. Maybe she couldn't and shouldn't protect them, maybe it was better for them to see and know. *Maybe innocence is a skin you must shed to build layers more resistant to the caustic truths of the world.* She wondered if she was living at the beginning of a new era, when the pale and protected began to live among the dark and the sorrowful, the angry multitudes of the south.

Behind them a door opened and Araceli and the boys turned around to see the woman from the first bungalow heading down the steps and walking toward them, with three giggling children trailing behind her.

ISABEL AGUILAR peeled back the curtain and spied on the lost strangers through the window of her small living room, which also doubled as the bedroom of her son and the Other Boy who lived with her. The three strangers sat on the curb, two white boys and a *mexicana* in a foul mood. Encounters with disoriented travelers were not unusual on Thirty-ninth Street, where Isabel's rented bungalow stood at the edge of a district of hurricane fencing and barbed wire, of HELP WANTED signs in Korean, Spanish, and Cantonese, where cloth was transformed into boutique T-shirts and steel was cut and solvents were mixed. When lost pedestrians reached Isabel's front step and contemplated the industrial horizon that began on her street, they realized they were in the wrong place and knocked on her door, twisting their faces into question marks: *"¿Y la Main, dónde está?"* "You know where my homie Ruben lives?" "Have any idea, honey, where I might find the United States Post Office?" Isabel answered the door for all of them, and sometimes opened the outer metal barrier, the better to hear their questions, even though she was a single mother living with her two children and the Other Boy who was not her son. She had been born in a town in the municipality of Sonsonate, El Salvador, a place of rusting railroad tracks where the green mushroom-cloud canopy of a single ceiba tree billowed over the central plaza and where neighbors knocked on your door expecting to be invited in.

The big Mexican woman sitting on the curb stood out among the parade of the lost on Thirty-ninth Street first for the startling photograph she presented as a calling card, an image of Isabel's bungalow before the floors sagged and the doors and windows were encased in steel, and second because the children she had with her were obviously not hers. Isabel detected a faint coloring of Oaxaca or Guatemala in their skin—perhaps she was their aunt or cousin. But there was something decidedly non–Latin American in the air of pampered curiosity with which they sized up Isabel and the bungalow. They reminded Isabel of the children she had cared for in Pasadena when she worked there one summer, boys who knew the abundance of expansive homes with unlocked doors and clutter-free stretches of hardwood floor that were swept and polished by women like her. Why was the Mexican woman dragging them around these parts, where the only white people she saw regularly were the policemen and the old man who collected the rent?

"What are you looking at?" asked the Other Boy behind her. "Why are you on my bed?" His name was Tomás, he was eleven, and he had lived with Isabel and her son and daughter for two years. The Other Boy was an orphan, and under strict orders to be quiet and grateful, and to bother her as little as possible, though he was constantly forgetting that last commandment. Isabel turned and gave him a scowl that involved a slight baring of her pewter-lined teeth.

"¡Cállate!" she snapped.

Tomás raised his eyebrows, smiled, and turned away, unfazed, returning to the movie he was watching with Héctor, Isabel's son and Tomás's best friend on earth, and with María Antonieta, Isabel's daughter.

Isabel found her natural provincial generosity once again pulling her toward the front door and down the stairs. These small-town instincts had gotten her into trouble before—the Other Boy being the principal reminder of this. But she sensed that outside on the curb there was a woman in a situation much like her own: alone with two children and the Other Boy and only the twice-monthly visits of the father of her children, Wandering-Eye Man, and his cash stipend to make the situation livable. Her ex had visited the previous weekend, which was why Isabel had had her nails and hair done, but all she had accomplished with that was to make his eyes fix on her for a heartbeat or two longer than usual.

When Isabel opened the door, Héctor, María Antonieta, and the Other Boy paused the movie they had been watching on their DVD player and the three of them followed her out the door and down the stairs.

Isabel leaned down and asked a question softly of Araceli. *"¿Tienen hambre? Tenemos hot dogs."*

PHOTO BY JUSTIN ANDREW MARKS

This anthology gratefully acknowledges receiving permission to reprint selections from some of the most wonderful writers on LA of the past two hundred years. But we'd also like to recommend a piece of comic literature that we aren't able to reprint because the fee for doing so far exceeds our budget. We're talking about twenty lines or so from a faux soap opera sketch from *Saturday Night Live.*

Oh well. Here's a link to the show's website, where you can see and hear the sketch. You'll have to take our word for it that it's fun to read, too.

ROUTE RIFF 2
"GLAD YOU CAME OVER"

THE CALIFORNIANS: STUART HAS CANCER

IN WHICH KARINA IS REALLY GLAD THAT DEVIN

came over but urges him to leave soon. Devin is working out his exit route when Stuart gets home early! Did he rush home because of suspicions about Karina and Devin's relationship? Maybe not, because he took Santa Monica instead of Wilshire and so made better time.

nbc.com/saturday-night-live/video/the-californians

"The old bus lines are really concrete," author Paul Beatty told *Los Angeles Review of Books* interviewer Evelyn McDonnell about his novel *The Sellout,* "...but the street names are from all over the place, some made up, some just streets I wanted to stick in there. I think I didn't want it to be like LA; I just wanted it to feel like it was LA." And so it does. The LA perceived from inside Beatty's protagonist's head is presented matter-of-factly, careful-ly, attentively. And yet it is so dense with images and allusions and layers that you're kind of saturated with a literary synesthesia, like people who experience numbers as colors or spoken dates as images floating at specific locations in the landscape. Comfortable? Maybe not. But you might want to be on the bus.

ROUTE RIFF 3
EXACT CHANGE

THE SELLOUT

PAUL BEATTY

MARPESSA LOOKED AT ME, THEN AT HER LONE WHITE
passenger, then back at me, and stopped the bus in the middle of a busy
intersection, flinging open the doors with all the civil servant courtesy she
could muster.

"Everybody who I don't know personally, get the fuck off the bus." "Everybody" being a lazy skateboarder and two kids who'd spent the past hour
necking like twisted rubber bands in the back, who quickly found themselves
in the middle of Rosecrans Avenue holding free transfer tickets that flapped
uselessly in the sea breeze. Miss Freedom Rider was about to join them when
Marpessa blocked her passage like Governor Wallace blocked the entrance to
the University of Alabama in 1963.

*In the name of the greatest people that have ever trod this earth, I draw the line
in the dust and toss the gauntlet before the feet of tyranny, and I say segregation
now, segregation tomorrow, segregation forever.*

"What's your name?" Marpessa asked as she cajoled the bus northbound
onto Las Mesas.

"Laura Jane."

"Well, Laura Jane, I don't know how you know this fertilizer smelling fool
right here, but I hope you like to party."

Unlike those expensive, staid, day-trip excursions to Catalina Island, the
impromptu four-wheel birthday party cruise up the Pacific Coast Highway

was free and jumping like a motherfucker. Our highway-next-to-the-ocean-liner had all the amenities: Open bar. Stomped-on aluminum can, whisk-broom shuffleboard. Casino gambling, which consisted of pitching pennies, dominoes. A coin-flip game called Get Like Me, and a disco lounge. Captain Marpessa womaned the helm, drinking and cursing like a pissed-off pirate. I filled in as First Mate, Purser, Deck Hand, Bartender, and DJ. We'd picked up some more passengers on the way when the bus pulled into the Jack in the Box drive-thru across the street from Malibu pier, cranking Whodini's "Five Minutes of Funk," and when we ordered fifty tacos and a shitload of sauce, the entire night shift quit on the spot and climbed aboard, aprons, paper hats, and all. If I had pen and paper and the bus had a bathroom, I would've posted another sign—ALL EMPLOYEES MUST WASH THEIR HANDS AND THEIR MINDS BEFORE RETURNING TO THEIR LIVES.

After night falls, once past Pepperdine University, where the highway narrows into a two-lane hill that stretches like a skate ramp to the stars, there isn't much light. Just the occasional flash of oncoming high beams, and, if you're lucky, a lonely bonfire on the sand, and the sheets of moonlight give the Pacific Ocean a glassy black obsidian sheen. It was on this same stretch of winding road that I first courted Marpessa. I bussed her on the cheek. She didn't flinch, which I interpreted as a good sign.

Although the bus cruise was bumping, Hominy had spent most of the ride standing in the middle of the dance floor, stubbornly holding on to the overhead bar and, by proxy, the history of American discrimination, but around Puerco Beach, Laura Jane had managed to coax him out of his ancient mindset by grinding her pelvic bone rhythmically against his backside and playing with his ears. "Freaking," we used to call it, and she pranced around Hominy, her hands overhead, caressing the beat. When the song ended, she shouldered her way toward the bow, the fuzz on her upper lip beaded with sweat. Goddamn, she was fine.

"Wicked party."

The radio buzzed to life, and a dispatcher said the word "whereabouts" in a concerned voice. Marpessa turned down the music, said something I couldn't hear, then blew a kiss into the receiver and switched off the radio. If New York is the City That Never Sleeps, then Los Angeles is the City That's Always Passed Out on the Couch. Once past Leo Carrillo, PCH begins to smooth out, and when the moon disappears behind the Santa Monica Mountains, painting the night sky pitch-black, if you listen closely you can hear two faint pops in fairly quick succession. The first is the sound of four million living-room television sets flickering off in unison, and the second is the sound of four million bedroom ones being powered on. Moviemakers and photographers often speak of the uniqueness of LA sunlight, the ways it pours itself across the sky, golden and sweet, like Vermeer, Monet, and breakfast honey all rolled into one. But the LA moonlight, or lack thereof rather, is just as special. When night falls, I mean really falls, the temperature drops twenty degrees and a total amniotic blackness blankets and comforts you like a lover making the bed while you're still in it, and that brief moment between television sets popping off and back on is the calm before the after-hours strip clubs in Inglewood open, before the cacophony of New Year's Eve gunshots rings out, before Santa Monica, Hollywood, Whittier, and Crenshaw Boulevards come slowly cruising to life, is when Angelenos take time to pause and reflect. To give thanks to the late-night joints in Koreatown. To Mariachi Square. To chili burgers and pastrami dip sandwiches. To Marpessa, peering through the windshield and squinting at the stars, driving by dead reckoning rather than simply following the road. The tires ground assuredly over the asphalt, the bus rolling through the stratosphere, and when she heard the second pop, Marpessa gave the go-ahead for more music, and before long, Hominy and the rest of the Jack in the Box ballet were again pirouetting in the aisle, singing out loud to Tom Petty.

"Where'd he find you?" Marpessa asked Laura Jane, her eyes still fixed on the Milky Way.

"He hired me."

"You a prostitute?"

"Damn near. Actress. Part-time submissive to pay the bills."

"Parts must be hard to come by if you have to do this shit." Marpessa cut her eyes at Laura Jane, bit her bottom lip, and turned her attention back to the celestial night.

"Have I ever seen you in anything?"

"I do mostly television commercials, but it's tough. Whenever I'm up for a part, the producers look at me like you just did and say, 'Not suburban enough,' which in the industry is code for 'too Jewish.'"

Sensing that Marpessa hadn't quite cleared her chakras during her LA moment of silence, Laura Jane pressed her pretty face cheek-to-cheek with Marpessa's jealous mug and together they studied themselves in the rearview mirror, looking like a pair of mismatched conjoined twins attached at the head. One middle-aged and black, the other young and white, sharing the same brain but not the same thought process. "Makes me wish I was black," the white twin said, smiling and running her hands over her darker sister's burning cheeks. "Black people get all the jobs."

Marpessa must've put the bus on autopilot, because her hands were off the steering wheel and around Laura Jane's neck. Not choking her, but pointedly straightening the collar of her dress, letting her evil twin know she was ready to pounce as soon as her side of the brain gave the okay. "Look, I doubt that black people get *all* the jobs. But even if they do, it's because Madison Avenue knows niggers spend a dollar and twenty cents of every dollar they earn on the crap they see on television. Let's take the standard luxury car commercial...."

Laura Jane nodded as if she were really listening, slyly slipping her arms around Marpessa and onto the steering wheel. For a second we veered across the double yellow lines, but she made a deft correction and gently guided the bus back into the passing lane.

"Luxury cars. You were saying?"

"The subtle message of the luxury car commercial is 'We here at Mercedes-Benz, BMW, Lexus, Cadillac, or whatever the fuck, are an equal-opportunity opportunist. See this handsome African-American male model behind the wheel? We'd like you, O holy, highly sought after white male consumer between the ages of thirty and forty-five, sitting in your recliner, we'd like you to spend your money and join our happy, carefree, prejudice-free world. A world where black men drive sitting straight up in their seats and not sunk so low and to the side you can see only the tops of their gleaming ball-peen heads.'"

"And what's so wrong with that?"

"But the subliminal message is 'Look, you lazy, fat, susceptible-to-marketing, poor excuse for a white man. You've indulged this thirty-second fantasy of a nigger dandy commuting from his Tudor castle in an aerodynamically designed piece of precision German engineering, so you'd better get your act together, bro, and stop letting these rack-and-pinion-steering, moon-roof, manufacturer's-suggested-retail-price-paying monkeys show you up and steal your piece of the American dream!'"

At mention of the American dream, Laura Jane stiffened and returned the conn to Marpessa. "I'm offended," she said.

"Because I used the word 'nigger'?"

"No, because you're a beautiful woman who just happens to be black, and you're far too smart not to know that it isn't race that's the problem but class."

Laura Jane planted a loud, wet smack on Marpessa's forehead and spun on her Louboutin heels to go back to work. I grabbed my love's arm in mid-swing, saving Laura Jane from a rabbit punch she never saw coming.

"You know why white people don't ever just happen to be white? Because they all think they've just happened to have been touched by God, that's why!"

I thumbed the lipstick print off Marpessa's angry forehead.

"And tell that class oppression garbage to the fucking Indians and the dodo birds. Talking about I should 'know better.' She's Jewish. *She* should know better."

"She didn't say she was Jewish. She said people *think* she looks Jewish."

"You are a fucking sellout. That's why I fucking dumped your ass. You never stick up for yourself. You're probably on her side."

Godard approached filmmaking as criticism, the same way Marpessa approached bus driving, but in any case, I thought Laura Jane had a point. Whatever Jewish people supposedly look like, from Barbra Streisand to the nominally Jewish-ish Whoopie Goldberg, you never see people in commercials that look "Jewish," just as you never see black people that come off as "urban" and hence "scary," or handsome Asian men, or dark-skinned Latinos. I'm sure those groups spend a disproportionate amount of their incomes on shit they don't need. And, of course, in the idyllic world of television advertisement, homosexuals are mythical beings, but you see more ads featuring unicorns and leprechauns than you do gay men and women. And maybe nonthreatening African-American actors are overrepresented on television. Their master's degrees from the Yale School of Drama and Shakespearean training having gone to waste, as they stand around barbecue pits delivering lines like "Prithee, homeboy. Forsooth, thou knowest that Budweiser is the King of Beers. Uneasy lies the frothy head that wears the crown." But if you really think about it, the only thing you absolutely never see in car commercials isn't Jewish people, homosexuals, or urban Negroes, it's traffic.

The bus slowed as Marpessa leaned into a left turn that took us off the highway and down a hidden, winding service road. We crept past a limestone outcropping, a set of rickety wooden coastal access stairs, and through an unused parking lot. From there, she downshifted, threw the bus in gear, and dune-buggied the vehicle directly onto the sand, where she parallel-parked with the horizon and, since the tide was up, in about a foot and a half of seawater.

"Don't worry, these things are like all-terrain vehicles and damn near amphibious. Between the mudslides and LA's shitty sewage system, a bus has to be able to slog through anything. If we'd used Metro buses to land on the beaches of Normandy on D-Day, World War II would've ended two years earlier."

The doors, both back and front, flew open, and the Pacific lapped lovingly at the bottom stairs, turning the bus into one of those Bora-Bora hotel rooms that sit on pylons fifty yards out to sea. I half expected to see a Jack in the Box service rep pull up on a Jet Ski delivering towels and a second round of sourdough burgers and vanilla shakes.

#MoreThanAHashtag, 2017

TO LIVE & THRIVE IN LA

JUSTIN ANDREW MARKS

Pictured here and in the following pages, marchers at the Women's March LA, including Dr. Melina Abdullah (above, holding phone)

I'm the type of person who has an abundance of empathy and respect for people, especially for Black women and those in the margins. I'm the type of person who's bothered by other people's pain and feels a deep joy seeing others happy. I'm the type of person who, growing up, was much more likely to get in a fight defending someone than standing up for myself. If I'm honest, I'm a romantic, and an idealist, and probably a bit naive. I think those attributes are shared by the types of people who change the world for the best. Maybe that means I'm a narcissist too.

Los Angeles is the entertainment capital of the world. It's the Hollywood Walk of Fame and the Staples Center. It's the Santa Monica Pier and Walt Disney Concert Hall. But it's also home to the world's largest jail system. In LA, Black people are eight percent of the population but forty percent of the prison population. LA is home to Skid Row, with one of the largest homeless populations in the country. There's a history here behind the silver screen. There's a disconnected presence. LA is the birthplace of the first chapter of what is now known as Black Lives Matter. "It's the city of angels and constant danger/South Central LA can't get no stranger" (Tupac Shakur, "To Live and Die in LA").

Photography mimics the way our brains freeze moments and emotions. In creating these images on January 22, 2017, I tried to use my empathy to connect intimate emotions and fleeting moments. I was surrounded by the daughters and granddaughters of fighters and survivors, along with people still in mourning. In the air, there were the sounds of drums and the loud affirmations from the crowd that Black Lives Matter; the smells of sweat and burning sage. Someone held a sign that read "This Is a Movement not a Moment." I'm reminded of the indelible words of Coretta Scott King: "Struggle is a never-ending process. Freedom is never really won, you earn it and win it in every generation." This, too, is Los Angeles.

—J.A.M.

Dignified Resistance, 2017

Make Up Your Mind, 2017

Not My President, 2017

Get It Done, 2017

Confidence and Cool, 2017

Pink Power, 2017

One Mic, 2017

Rise, 2017

STEVE MARTIN. Excerpt from *L.A. Story.* Copyright ©1987 by 40 Share Productions, Inc. Used by permission of Grove/Atlantic, Inc. Any third-party use of this material, outside of this publication, is prohibited. http://www.groveatlantic.com.

WILLIAM HEATH DAVIS. From *Seventy-five Years in California* (San Francisco: J. Howell, 1929).

HUGO REID. From the July 24, 1852, issue of the *Los Angeles Star (La Estrella de Los Angeles).* Available at USC Digital Library (http://digitallibrary.usc.edu) in the online collection of the 500 issues of the Huntington Library collection.

ARNA BONTEMPS. Extract from *God Sends Sunday* (New York: Washington Square Press, 2005). Copyright ©1931, 1959 by Arna Bontemps. Reprinted by permission of Harold Ober Associates Incorporated. http://haroldober.com.

VICTORIA DAILEY. "Culture, Books & Booze." Copyright ©2018 Victoria Dailey. http://victoriadailey.com.

CARLOS BULOSAN. From *America Is in the Heart: A Personal History* (Seattle: University of Washington Press, 1973, 2014). Originally published by Harcourt, Brace and Company, 1946. http://www.washington.edu/uwpress/.

ROBERT LANDAU. "Photo Essay: LA Obscura." Photographs and essay copyright © Robert Landau. Used by permission. http://www.robertlandau.com.

SUSAN SONTAG. "Pilgrimage" from *Debriefing: Collected Stories* by Susan Sontag, edited by Benjamin Taylor. Copyright ©2017 David Rieff. First published in *The New Yorker*, December 21, 1987. Reprinted by permission of Farrar, Straus and Giroux. https://us.macmillan.com/fsg/.

CLANCY SIGAL. From *Black Sunset: Hollywood Sex, Lies, Glamour, Betrayal, and Raging Egos* (Berkeley: Soft Skull Press, 2016). Copyright ©2016 by Clancy Sigal. Reprinted by permission. Soft Skull Press, an imprint of Counterpoint. https://softskull.com.

EVE BABITZ. "Frozen Looks" from *Eve's Hollywood* (New York: New York Review Books, 2015). Copyright ©1972, 1974 Eve Babitz. Reprinted by permission. https://www.nyrb.com.

VENICE ARTS. "Photo Essay: Venice Skate Park Through the Eyes of Youth." Photographs copyright © Venice Arts. Essay copyright ©2017 Elysa Voshell. http://www.venicearts.org.

VIN SCULLY. Transcript of Vin Scully's call of the ninth inning of the Los Angeles Dodgers and Chicago Cubs game played on September 9, 1965, reprinted with permission of Mr. Scully, the Los Angeles Dodgers, and Major League Baseball Properties, Inc.

DAN BERN. "The Ballad of Dave and Eddie" first published in *Zyzzyva* VII, no. 2, summer 1991. Copyright ©1991 by Dan Bern. Reprinted by permission of the author. http://danbern.com.

VICTOR M. VALLE AND MARY LAU VALLE. "Children of Maya-guel" from *Recipe of Memory: Five Generations of Mexican Cuisine.* Copyright ©1995 by Victor Valle and Mary Lau Valle. Reprinted by permission of The New Press. www.thenewpress.com.

CECIL CASTELLUCCI. Excerpt from *Beige* (Somerville, MA: Candlewick Press, 2009). Copyright ©2007 Cecil Castellucci. Reproduced by permission of the publisher, Candlewick Press. http://www.candlewick.com.

HÉCTOR TOBAR. Excerpt from *The Barbarian Nurseries* (New York: Farrar, Straus and Giroux, 2011). Copyright ©2011 Héctor Tobar. Reprinted by permission of Farrar, Straus and Giroux. https://us.macmillan.com/fsg/.

PAUL BEATTY. Excerpt from "Exact Change" from *The Sellout* (New York: Farrar, Straus and Giroux, 2015). Copyright ©2015 Paul Beatty. Reprinted by permission of Farrar, Straus and Giroux. https://us.macmillan.com/fsg/.

JUSTIN ANDREW MARKS. "Photo Essay: To Live and Thrive in LA." Photographs and essay copyright ©2017 Justin Andrew Marks.

SOURCES & ACKNOWLEDGMENTS (IN ORDER OF APPEARANCE)

Our contributors hail from many eras of LA literary life and write from many different vantage points. They're all in good company.

EVE BABITZ is the author of four novels, including *Eve's Hollywood, LA Woman, Sex and Rage: Advice to Young Ladies Eager for a Good Time,* a book of short stories, and two books of non-fiction that chronicle some of her cultural enthusiasms. She has contributed articles, essays, and short stories to such magazines as *L.A. Style, Rolling Stone, Vogue, Cosmopolitan, Esquire, Westways,* and *Newsweek.*

PAUL BEATTY, LA-born author of *The Sellout,* is the first American writer to receive the Man Booker Prize, which he did for that novel. He also received the National Book Critics Circle Award for fiction in 2016 and was the Grand Poetry Slam Champion in 1990. He has written three other novels, *White Boy Shuffle, Tuff,* and *Slumberland,* and edited *Hokum,* an anthology of African-American humor. Beatty is currently a professor at Columbia University.

DAN BERN is a singer-songwriter who tours frequently and has released eighteen albums. He collaborated with Emmylou Harris on a duet for his album *Drifter* and on another for an off-Broadway production directed by Jonathan Demme. He has written songs for movies and television and wrote a song with Hunter S. Thompson. His album *Breathe* won 2007 Best Folk/Singer-Songwriter at the Sixth Annual Independent Music Awards.

ARNA BONTEMPS was the Harlem Renaissance writer best known for his novel *God Sends Sunday,* published in 1931 and adapted by him and the poet Countee Cullen into the play *St. Louis Woman,* later turned into a musical. Born in 1902 in Louisiana, he moved with his family to Los Angeles when he was three and was educated in California before taking a job teaching in New York. Bontemps wrote works of historical fiction about slave revolts as well as histories for young readers, and he published several anthologies of Black poetry and folklore.

CARLOS BULOSAN was one of thousands of Pilipino Americans who fled deprivation created by colonization only to face extreme poverty in America. He arrived as a teenager in 1930 and survived hunger, homelessness, racial violence, tuberculosis, and intolerable working conditions in canneries and fields. He became a labor organizer and published poetry and fiction. Bulosan was best known for his 1943 essay for *Saturday Evening Post* on hunger, part of a series based on FDR's "Four Freedoms" speech.

CECIL CASTELLUCCI was an indie rocker in Canada and LA in the 1990s. Now she divides her time as a self-described "authoress" between writing graphic novels (DC Comics's *Shade, the Changing Girl; The P.L.A.I.N. Janes*) and YA novels (*Boy Proof, The Queen of Cool, Tin Star, Moving Target: A Princess Leia Adventure*). She hosts the monthly Teen Author Reading Series at the LAPL Central Library and is the YA editor for the *Los Angeles Review of Books.* Her awards include the California Book Award Gold Medal for *Grandma's Gloves,* illustrated by Julia Denos; a Shuster Award (Best Canadian Comic Book Writer) for *The P.L.A.I.N. Janes;* and the Sunburst Award for *Tin Star.*

VICTORIA DAILEY is a writer, curator, antiquarian bookseller, and lecturer. The co-author of *LA's Early Moderns: Art, Architecture, Photography* and author of *Songs in the Key of Los Angeles:*

Sheet Music from the Collection of the Los Angeles Public Library, Dailey contributes humor and essays to *The New Yorker* and *L.A. Review of Books*. Her recent exhibitions include *Tea & Morphine: Women in Paris 1880–1914* (Hammer Museum, 2014) and *Piety & Perversity: The Palms of Los Angeles* (William Andrews Clark Memorial Library, 2015). She has also published such books as the 1996 limited edition of *Wasp*, a one-act play by Steve Martin, illustrated by Martin Mull.

WILLIAM HEATH DAVIS wrote a memoir in 1889 looking back on his early years in California from a position of wealth and achievement. Born in Hawaii and part Hawaiian, he visited California in the early 1830s, settled there in 1838, and married Maria de Jesus Estudillo, daughter of the San Leandro land grantee, which connected him to Californio society. His business, political, and social activities carried Davis up and down the state, and he is known for being both a founder of San Diego's New Town and a San Francisco city councilman.

ROBERT LANDAU has published five books of photography: *Rock n' Roll Billboards of the Sunset Strip, Billboard Art, Outrageous LA, Airstream*, and *Hollywood Poolside*. His work has been shown at museums and galleries worldwide, including the Grammy Museum, Palm Springs Desert Museum, San Francisco Museum of Modern Art, and Brand Gallery. His editorial photography appears in dozens of publications, including *Los Angeles, Forbes, National Geographic, Rolling Stone, Stern Magazine, Time*, and *Travel & Leisure*. His father owned the influential 1960s Felix Landau Gallery in Los Angeles.

JUSTIN ANDREW MARKS is an LA-based scholar, activist, and artist dedicated to challenging and dismantling systems of oppression to set in place societal transformation and the liberation of Black people. He helped incubate the Brothers, Sons, Selves Coalition of ten grassroots LA organizations; has been in service in California and Kampala, Uganda, with the Prison Education Program; mobilized system-involved youth to pass the Safe Neighborhoods & Schools Act in California; and led workshops for parents, youth, and staff. His photographic style is inspired by the montages in films from his favorite cinematographer, Ernest Dickerson.

CONTRIBUTORS

STEVE MARTIN, the hyphenate's hyphenate, is an award-winning banjo player whose literary works include novels, plays, screenplays, essay collections, and a collection of tweets. Angelenos of the right era saw him onstage as a comedian before he made it to *The Tonight Show*.

HUGO REID was a Scot who settled in Los Angeles in the early nineteenth century. A naturalized Mexican citizen who spoke Spanish and English and was known by his Mexican name, Don Perfecto, he was married to Victoria Bartolomea, a Gabrielino/Tongva woman. They were the first private owners of Rancho Santa Anita. Reid is known for his letters about local indigenous people to LA's first newspaper, the *Los Angeles Star (La Estrella de Los Angeles)*, some of which have recently become more easily accessible in their original form. This is thanks to the USC Digital Library collection of the 500 issues of *The Star* from the Huntington Library holdings.

VIN SCULLY began as a broadcaster with the Dodgers in 1950 before the team moved to LA, but Dodger Stadium is the place that resounds with his voice, and fans are still pining for it on their car radios. Not all of the nearly 10,000 Dodger games he called before his 2016 retirement were recorded. The ninth inning (not the whole game) of Sandy Koufax's perfect game, however, was captured and made into a phonograph record that was sold as a souvenir at the stadium.

CLANCY SIGAL, as he would write about in his book, *A Woman of Uncertain Character: The Amorous and Radical Adventures of My Mother Jennie (Who Always Wanted to Be a Respectable Jewish Mom) by Her Bastard Son*, was born to union organizers in Chicago. He lived in Los Angeles in the 1950s and again from 1984 until his death in 2017. His biography is stuffed with famous names and historic moments, and it's quite a tale. A prolific writer of books, journalism, and screenplays, Sigal was a journalism professor at USC. His best-known book, *Going Away*, was nominated for a National Book Award, and he received the Lifetime Achievement Award from PEN USA in 2007.

SUSAN SONTAG was one of America's most influential public intellectuals in the latter half of the twentieth century and an LGBTQ and feminist icon. Best known for her book-length essays (including *On Photography, On Camp, Against Interpretation,* and *Illness as Metaphor*) and her articles on war, photography and media, AIDS, and illness, she also published four novels and wrote and directed films and plays. Sontag attended high school in Los Angeles.

HÉCTOR TOBAR, the son of Guatemalan immigrants, is an LA native and a professor of journalism at the University of Oregon. He writes for *The New Yorker, The New York Times*, and other publications and was for many years a writer for the *Los Angeles Times,* for which he was part of the 1992 reporting team that won a Pulitzer Prize for coverage of the city's civil unrest. Tobar is the author of two works of fiction, *The Barbarian Nurseries* and *The Tattooed Soldier*, and two nonfiction titles, *Deep Down Dark: The Untold Stories of 33 Men Buried in a Chilean Mine and the Miracle That Set Them Free* and *Translation Nation: Defining a New American Identity in the Spanish-Speaking United States.*

VICTOR M. and MARY LAU VALLE are co-authors of the book *Recipe of Memory: Five Generations of Mexican Cuisine.* Victor Valle is a professor emeritus in the Cal Poly San Luis Obispo Ethnic Studies department. He was a member of the reporting team that won a Pulitzer Prize in 1984 for the series "Southern California's Latino Community" for the *Los Angeles Times.* At the newspaper, he wrote frequently about music and the culture of food. He is also the author or co-author of the books *Latino Metropolis* and *City of Industry: Genealogies of Power in Southern California.*

ELYSA VOSHELL is the associate director of gallery and public programs at Venice Arts, a nonprofit organization whose mission is to ignite, expand, and transform the lives of LA's low-income youth through photography and film education. A curator, writer, and artist working primarily in photography, printmaking, book arts, and installation, she manages the Venice Arts exhibitions, which feature the work of professional, participant, and youth artists.

PHOTO BY JUSTIN ANDREW MARKS